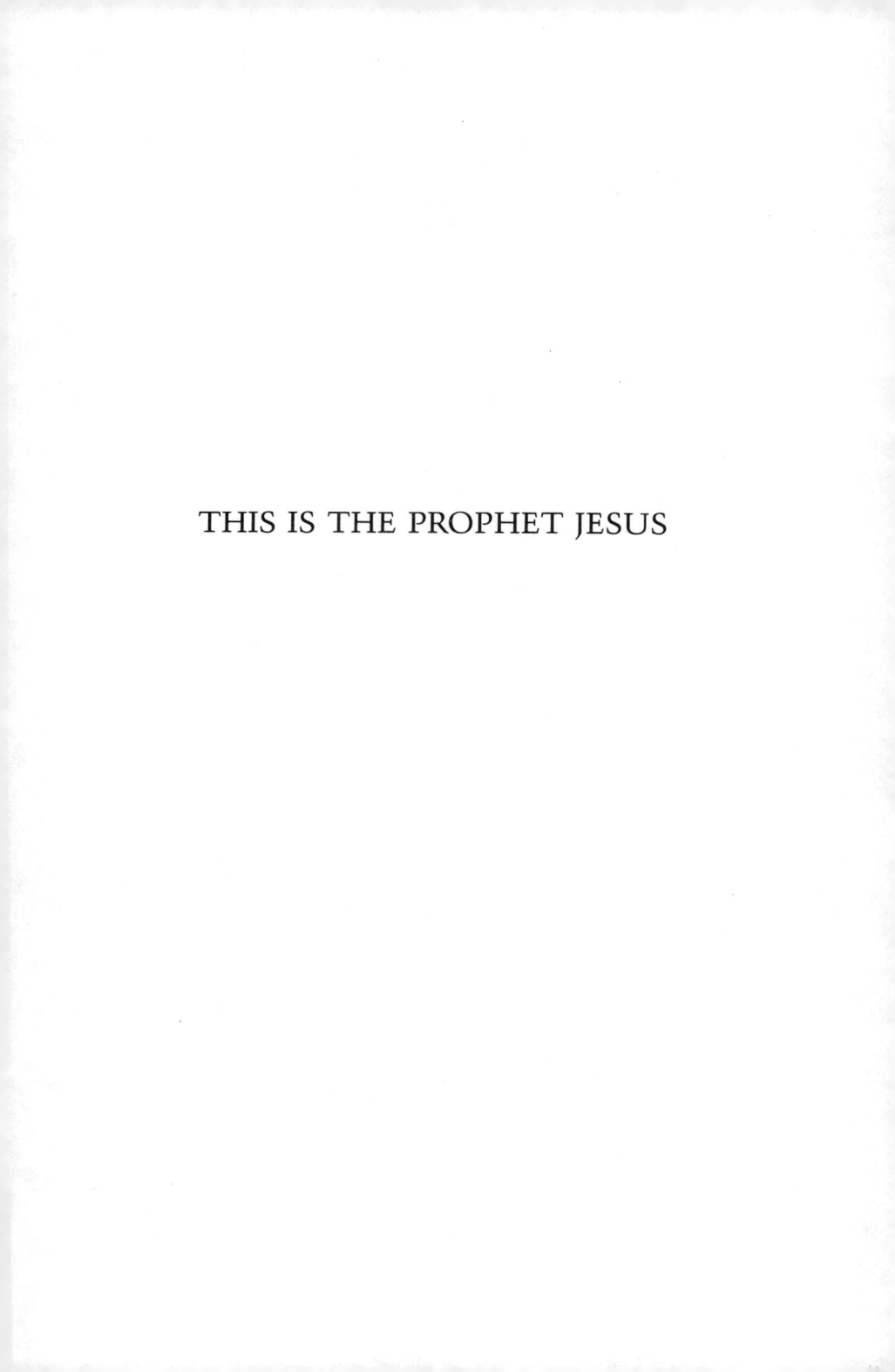

THIS IS THE PROPHET JESUS

THIS IS THE PROPHET JESUS

*An Evolutionary Approach
To His Teaching*

by
Fred S. Howes

DeVorss & Company, Publisher
Box 550—Marina del Rey—California 90291

Note: The lines in biblical Greek shown on the cover are from an ancient copy of the Lukan Gospel. This is Jesus' Paradox (Luke 17:33) which reveals his secret for the attainment of fullness of life. It is discussed in § 35, page 93 of this book.

Copyright © April 27, 1982, Fred S. Howes. All rights reserved. No part of this publication may be reproduced by any means without prior permission in writing from the author.

ISBN: 0-87516-497-8
Library of Congress Catalog Card Number: 82-072741

Printed in the United States of America

To The Memory of
Henry Burton Sharman, Ph.D.
1865–1953
Great Scholar, Great Teacher,
Warm Friend

CONTENTS

About the Author   xv
Why Study the Life of Jesus—
    Henry Burton Sharman.   xviii
Acknowledgments.   xx
Introduction—The Fate of the
    Religious Innovator.   1
How the Gospel Material for this Study
    was Selected.   25

PART I
JESUS THE TEACHER

1 Activity of John and its Relation to Jesus.   29
  § 1. Statement of the Work of John.
  § 2. Baptism of Jesus by John.
  § 3. Withdrawal of Jesus to the Wilderness.

2 Beginnings of the Public Activity of Jesus.   38

§ 4. Jesus Teaches in Nazareth.
§ 5. Jesus Teaches in Capernaum.
§ 6. Jesus and Mental Cases.
§ 7. Jesus Wins Fisherman Followers.
§ 8. Jesus Teaches in Galilee.

3 Development of Opposition to Jesus.   43

§ 9. Criticism of Free Forgiveness for Sins.
§ 10. Criticism for Association with Sinners.
§ 11. Criticism of Attitude Toward Fasting.
§ 12. Criticism for Working on the Sabbath.
§ 13. Culmination of Criticism of Jesus.
§ 14. Attitude of Jesus Toward Criticism.

4 Definition of Standards of Righteousness by Jesus.   50

§ 15. Widespread Fame of Jesus.
§ 16. Appointment of Twelve Associates.
§ 17. Discourse on Standards of Righteousness.

5 Contemporary Opinions about the Worth of Jesus.   62

§ 18. Opinion of a Roman Centurian.
§ 19. Opinion of John the Baptist.

§ 20. Opinion of a Sinner versus Opinion of a Pharisee.

§ 21. Opinion of the Friends of Jesus.

§ 22. Opinion of the Religious Leaders.

6 The Mystery of the Kingdom of God.   70

§ 23. Basis of Real Relationship to Jesus.

§ 24. Discourse on the Kingdom of God.

7 Activity on Tours of Jesus and Disciples.   79

§ 25. Fear versus Faith.

§ 26. Jesus Teaches at Nazareth.

§ 27. Disciples Tour in Galilee.

§ 28. Fate of John the Baptist.

§ 29. Report of Associates on their Tour.

8 Demand of Pharisees for Conformity and Credentials.   85

§ 30. Concerning Traditions About Defilement.

§ 31. Pharisees Demand Signs from Jesus.

§ 32. The Leaven of the Pharisees.

9 Forecast of Conflict with Jerusalem Authorities.   91

§ 33. Opinion of Disciples About Jesus.

§ 34. Jesus Forecasts Events at Jerusalem.

§ 35. Some Costs of Discipleship.
§ 36. The Problem of Tribute Payment.
§ 37. Teaching on Greatness.
§ 38. Teaching on Tolerance.
§ 39. Teaching on Forgiveness.
§ 40. Parable on Forgiveness.

10 Departure from Galilee for Jerusalem.   103

§ 41. General Statement of Journey.
§ 42. Teaching on Tolerance.
§ 43. Some Tests of Discipleship.
§ 44. The Way of Eternal Life.
§ 45. The Definition of Neighbor.
§ 46. Many Things versus One Thing.
§ 47. Elements of Prevailing Prayer.
§ 48. Limitations of Exorcism.
§ 49. Basis of Real Relationship to Jesus.

11 Deep Feeling and Direct Teaching.   116

§ 50. Effects of the Mission of Jesus.
§ 51. The Signs of the Times.
§ 52. Warnings of National Disaster.
§ 53. Teaching about Reliance on Wealth.
§ 54. Saying on Light and Darkness.

§ 55. Limits of the Kingdom of God.
§ 56. Forecast of his Death by Jesus.
§ 57. Teaching in Criticism of Anxiety.
§ 58. Teaching at the Table of a Pharisee.
§ 59. The Cost of Discipleship.

12 Many Truths Taught in Parables. 129

§ 60. Parable on the Worth of Sinners.
§ 61. God versus Mammon.
§ 62. Parable on the Futility of Duty.
§ 63. Several Sayings of Jesus.
§ 64. Parable on Deferred Judgment.
§ 65. Time of the Kingdom of God.
§ 66. Parable on Importunity in Prayer.
§ 67. Several Sayings of Jesus.
§ 68. Parable on the Basis of Justification.

13 Teaching and Journeying on to Jerusalem. 141

§ 69. Teaching about Divorce.
§ 70. Relation of Possessions to Eternal Life.
§ 71. Parable on the Basis of Reward.
§ 72. Teaching on Standards of Greatness.
§ 73. The Rich Publican of Jericho.
§ 74. Time of the Kingdom of God.

14 Challenge of the Jerusalem Leaders
by Jesus. 153

§ 75. Jesus Enters Jerusalem as Popular Leader.

§ 76. Jesus Casts Commerce from the Temple.

§ 77. Jesus Teaches in the Temple.

§ 78. Jewish Rulers Challenge the Authority of Jesus.

§ 79. Parables in Condemnation of Jewish Leaders.

§ 80. Efforts to Accumulate Evidence Against Jesus.

15 Discourse in Condemnation of Scribes and Pharisees. 170

§ 81. Discourse in Condemnation of Scribes and Pharisees.

16 Discourse on Events of the Future. 175

§ 82. Discourse on Events of the Future.

§ 83. Teaching by Jesus in Jerusalem.

17 Final Hours of Jesus with His Disciples. 186

§ 84. Conspiracy for the Arrest of Jesus.

§ 85. The Passover with the Disciples.

§ 86. Withdrawal to the Mount of Olives.

§ 87. At the Place Named Gethsemane.

§ 88. Betrayal and Arrest of Jesus.

18 Judicial Trials and Crucifixion of Jesus.   193

§ 89. The Trial before the Jewish Authorities.

§ 90. The Trial before the Roman Authorities.

§ 91. The Crucifixion of Jesus.

PART II

*Information Supplementary to Part I
And Some Reflections on Jesus' Teaching.*

19 Definitions of Some Words Used
in this Book.   205

20 Judaism in the Time of Jesus.   210

21 Revolts of the Jews Against Rome,
AD 6–73.   213

22 The Effect of Emotional Arousal on
Moral Discrimination.   216

23 Messianic (Christ) Concepts in Relation
to Jesus.   219

24 Anthropomorphisms in the Language
of Religion.   227

25 The Meaning of the Phrase *Will of God*. 233

Bibliography. 243

Note: References throughout this book are indicated as follows:

[ ] refers to Chapters in Part II.
( ) refers to books listed in the Bibliography.
§ refers to sections of the Biblical material in Part I.

For purposes of continuity in this book, the paragraphs from Dr. Sharman's book *Jesus as Teacher* have been re-numbered to be in consecutive order; the paragraph captions have not been changed.

ABOUT THE AUTHOR

My childhood was spent on a farm; my adolescence in a city. At 20 I was a soldier; at 23, an industrial worker; at 24, an engineering undergraduate. At 33 when I had earned a Ph.D. I returned to my University and department as a lecturer and so began a long and varied academic career.

My introduction to the teaching of Jesus was quite fortuitous. John MacKay, a veteran like myself of the first World War and Warden of the dormitory in which I lived, invited me to join with a small group of students which was about to begin a comparative study of the Synoptic Gospels—Matthew, Mark, Luke. Somewhat reluctantly I accepted, but truth is I found that one-evening-a-week spent exploring those ancient documents a fascinating adventure. So much so that I continued with it throughout my undergraduate years and beyond.

Soon after graduation I was able to attend a summer seminar on the *Records of the Life of Jesus*, conducted by Dr. Henry Burton Sharman, a distinguished New Testament scholar. As the saying goes (and it was said of me), I was *hooked* on Jesus.

Shortly after becoming a member of the teaching staff of my university, I began to meet with student groups one evening a week to lead the discussion in a comparative study of the Synoptic Gospels as was done by Dr. Sharman in his summer seminars. The opportunity to participate in a critical study of *The Records* proved to be quite popular with some of the more thoughtful students for, apart from the interest of digging through the layers of accretion that overlay what could be authentic words of Jesus, there was the strong motivation supplied by the insight gained from some of Jesus' sayings.

During the early '30's my summer vacations were spent as Factotem at Camp Minnesing where Dr. Sharman held his study seminars. In 1935 I was asked to lead a similar summer seminar at a camp in the American South West and did so for a month each summer until 1940.

Extended over many years, this experience of participating in group discussion—comparing, analyzing, probing those 2000 year old documents (and ourselves) for meanings; sharing insights and helping one another avoid the blindness imposed by preconceptions—resulted in my learning a great deal about the Synoptic reports and, more importantly, about the mind of Jesus. And, as I gained insight into the meaning and relevance of Jesus' teaching, there came a clearer perception also of the constraints imposed by the presuppositions of Christian mythology.

Naturally my training and experience as an engineer was an important factor in determining my approach to the study of these narrative accounts of Jesus' life. No less important was my long association with Dr. Sharman—for me a most fortunate circumstance.

People who write books do so for a variety of reasons and of course from a variety of points of view. As to point of view—that has emerged, as Schweitzer said, *Aus meinem Leben und Denken*. We learn from experience else we learn not at all and what we have so learned we may not later disavow. We must be honest with ourselves.

The impulse to write this book now had its genesis in a growing concern about the present situation in our society—the general disarray of institutional religion; the wide-spread effort to denigrate science and its method; the proliferation of panaceas—psuedo-science, psuedo-religion, occultism, which offer illusory escape from the complexities of modern life.

The Prophet Jesus had an alternative to all this confusion. His solution to the problem of insecurity, when phrased in present-day language, is intelligible and adequte for modern man. That is what this book is about. It is intended for intelligent, educated people who are looking for a way to live meaningful lives in a seemingly meaningless world.

Fred S. Howes, Ph.D., Eng.
Emeritus Professor of Electrical Engineering,
McGill University,
Montreal, May 1982.

WHY STUDY THE LIFE OF JESUS

... We should study the life of Jesus because we get from his life and teaching ultimate principles, not prescriptions. We need men who try to simplify life—not a new code of morals. Jesus is one who gave us principles and not prescriptions. What we want is principles. A principle for our relation to our fellow men—valid, workable, possible, always easy to apply, marked by the finest idealism, and yet practicable. A principle for our relation to God—all comprehensive though all-exacting. It is worthwhile to study Jesus to get all these secrets. They are not all on the surface. We have to work for them. They are written in the Book. Study it and let Him speak.*

—Henry Burton Sharman (37)

* This paragraph is from a transcript of an address given by Dr. Sharman to the Brome Lake Conference in 1918. It was printed in "The Canadian Student Magazine" that year, and in 1922 it was reprinted in "The Student World."

NOTE Re. SEX DISCRIMINATION

The Jewish bible and the New Testament were written in a patriarchal time and therefore, understandably, biblical language referring to God is masculine. Traditionally, Christian theologians have maintained this oulook with the result that "female" has, in our culture, continued to mean something inferior to "male."

In this book, let it be understood that men and women are regarded and are intended to be treated as "persons" rather than as members of the opposite sex. Thus the word "man" is to be read as generic for humankind and the personal pronouns as interchangeable—he/she; him/her; his/hers. For *good man* read *good person*.

ACKNOWLEDGMENTS

First of all I want to say that I am deeply indebted to the late Henry Burton Sharman for his friendship over many years; for his books, and for the opportunity to attend many of his "Records Seminars" at Camp Minnesing in Algonquin Park, Ontario. Whatever understanding I have of the mind of Jesus I owe largely to Sharman's relentless prodding and probing questions.

Second, I am grateful to Sequoia Seminar Inc., Palo Alto, CA., present holders of the copyright to Dr. Sharman's books, for permission, generously given, for the use of the textual material of Sharman's "Jesus as Teacher."

I am indebted also to the following publishers for permission to quote from their books:

G. and C. Merriam, Co., Publishers of the Merriam-Webster Dictionaries, for a number of definitions from Webster's Third International Dictionary, 1976.

Cambridge University Press for a number of quotations from Sir Charles Sherrington's "Man on His Nature," paperback edition, 1975.

Columbia University Press for two items from Columbia Encyclopedia, Third Edition, 1963.

The Student Christian Movement of Canada for quotations from "This One Thing—a Tribute to Henry Burton Sharman," 1959.
Abingdon Press for two items from "The Handbook of Christian Theology" by Halberson and Cohen, 1957.
And finally my thanks to the many who have helped along the way: Mrs. Patten (A.J.), friend over many years who, *mirabile dictu*, managed to produce clean, typed copy from my largely illegible script; Peggy Pond Church, Bob and Lois Chipman, Allie V. Douglas, Martyn and Molly Estall, Beth Fowler, James and Caroline Gibson, Gwen Grant, Frances Warnecke Horn, George and Ruth Haythorne, Eric and Mary Jacobsen, Lloyd and Jessie Jones, Paul McCullagh, Mac and Mary Joyce McGoodwin, Wendell MacLeod, Earl Willmott, my sister Helen, who read the manuscript for spelling, grammar and punctuation lapses, and my wife Margaret who read and reread the manuscript and contributed greatly to the clarity by questions and suggestions at many points. My special thanks to Bill Gibson whose editorial expertness, voluntarily contributed, supplied a much needed overall treatment of the manuscript.

Montreal, June 1982.

INTRODUCTION

The Fate of the Religious Innovator

From time to time, all down the ages, an outstanding individual has appeared bearing fresh insight concerning the human condition. He has tried to share these discoveries with his contemporaries but on the whole the new concepts were either unwelcome or not well understood though the quality of life of the person was recognized and appreciated by many.

After the leader was gone, an effort was made by some of his followers to recall what they could of his teaching. However, within a generation or two, the essential point of the message, not clearly grasped when the teacher was alive, was largely forgotten or distorted and obscured. The innovator, his personality exalted and explanations of his uniqueness invented, became, in time, an object of veneration, even worship.

Examples of this growth of a mythology are Buddhism and Christianity. But Buddha was not a Buddhist: no more was Jesus a Christian.

Jesus, a Jew, was born in Nazareth, Galilee, probably about 3 BC. His public career began about AD 27 and he was executed—perhaps a year later—

by the Roman Governor at the instigation of the Jewish religious leaders. During that brief period as a public figure, Jesus created such a disturbance that the effects are, in one form or another, still with us—and likely to be.

Obviously this *Jesus Phenomenon* called for an explanation and, as it happened, one was available, ready made. The Jewish people believed [20] that God, their king, would send an agent, the Messiah (Christ) to establish his Kingdom and they were convinced that the arrival of this emissary was imminent. This notion of a Messiah, a redeemer, sent by God (10) was, it seems, not unique to the Jews, but has occurred among different peoples throughout history and may reflect a universal psychological pattern. Be that as it may, almost from the outset of his public career, some of Jesus' followers found in him a fit candidate for the Messianic role and promptly began to apply that title to him.

Whether Jesus accepted or rejected this application of the Christ title to him, some explanation of this extraordinary person is as necessary now as it was in AD 30. Can the true explanation of how Jesus became the person he was be found in the meager records of his life if we look at them *objectively?*

Reports about the life of Jesus have come down to us in the form of four small books—Mark, Luke, Matthew and John, probably written in AD 60, 80, 85 and 90-95 respectively (2). Although, as Luke indicates in his Preface: Lk 1:1-4 (ERV 1881):

FORASMUCH as many have taken in hand to draw up a narrative concerning those matters which have been fulfilled among us, even as they delivered them unto us, which from the beginning were eyewitnesses and ministers of the word, it seemed good to me also, having traced the course of all things accurately from the first, to write unto thee an orderly account, most excellent Theophilus; so that thou mightest know the certainty concerning the things wherein thou wast instructed.

there were other, earlier collections of the sayings of Jesus; the four books we have are those selected by the Church Fathers and made the official record.

The first three of these books are narrative accounts of the *Jesus Story*. The fourth book, John, is different—more of a philosophical appreciation of Jesus' teaching, differing in language, order and outlook from the other three (35).

Any search for the *Jesus of History* must be made in the narrative accounts of his life—the Synoptic Gospels. And if we are to study these books comparatively, they must be arranged in parallel columns so that they may be looked at together. One such arrangement is Sharman's *Records of the Life of Jesus* (3).

When we examine closely these three narrative accounts, we find many likenesses and differences. Mark, the shortest of the books, was an original source. Matthew and Luke were the work of editors. Apparently both Matthew and Luke possessed Mark, for all but a few verses of Mark are found in one or the other of them. Most of it is found in both. In Luke it is in the same order as in Mark; in Matthew it is in the same order except for chapters 8, 9 and 10.

Matthew and Luke evidently possessed two other written sources in common, one dealing with Jesus' Galilean ministry, the other dealing with Jesus' sojourn in Peraea on his way to Jerusalem.

As with his treatment of Mark, Luke respected the order of these other documents when he incorporated them into his book. Matthew on the other hand, though he departed little from the order of Mark, distributed the material found in these other sources throughout his book, placing it in one or the other of his many discourses in whatever context appeared to him to be suitable.

Thus from the outset, we find the literary principles and editorial policy of the author Matthew differing markedly from those of the author Luke. Their respective goals differed. Luke was concerned to *trace the course of all things accurately from the first* and to prepare an orderly account of what probably happened as he was able to discover it through his research. Matthew was influenced in his treatment of the available material by the preconception that Jesus spoke in discourses and he was preoccupied throughout with the necessity of proving, beyond a doubt, that Jesus was the Christ of Jewish tradition.

Thus we find in Matthew seven discourses located wherever he found a suitable setting or nucleus in Mark. Luke has only two discourses and Mark only one. Further, we find in Matthew a continual use of Old Testament quotations introduced always with the purpose of showing that Jesus was conscious of himself as the Christ and that his career was in fact the literal fulfilment of prophecy. Practically nothing of the sort is found in the other two books.

In addition to Mark, the Galilean and Peraean documents, Matthew and Luke each possessed sources not available to or at least not used by the other. One used only by Luke deals with the activity of Jesus in Jerusalem during the final phases of his life. A valuable written source used by Matthew alone, appears to have consisted mainly of teaching material. Much of the content of *the Sermon on the Mount* comes from this document.

Over and above the written material, Matthew and Luke each appear to have had access to oral tradition—stories about Jesus which were circulating at the time they wrote but which had not yet appeared in written form. The *birth stories* and the material dealing with events subsequent to the death of Jesus appear to have had this origin. Mark has no birth stories and they are also absent from the Galilean document which records the early history of Jesus' public activity. Again, Mark ends with the discovery of the empty tomb, whereas Matthew and Luke recount tales of post-resurrection appearances. However, in these parts of their books, Matthew and Luke have practically nothing in common. Luke's birth stories and post-resurrection reports are both much more extensive than Matthew's and differ in all essential details. It would appear, therefore, that these stories were still, at that time, in a very fluid state; that they had only recently come into being and that these editors took them as they found them. Their value for us is largely in what they reveal of the current hopes and expectations, political and religious, and in the clue which the post-resurrection appearances provide for our understanding of the growth of the subsequent Christian tradition [23].

This brief comparison of the composition of the synoptic records makes it obvious that we are dealing with human documents each of which, though different, purports to present a true account of Jesus' public career. Actually of course due to the circumstances of their origin and transmission, these reports were bound to contain interpretations inserted to suit the preconceptions of the narrators. The people of Jesus' day were in many ways very much like us; they saw what they wanted to see, they heard what they wanted to hear, and they remembered what intrigued them. And since there were no short-hand typists to keep the record straight and, even less, cassette recorders to store the voice—*ipsissima verba*—but only memory and, after many years, that but dimly, the surprising thing is that we have so much that is probably authentic.

As we have seen, all the information we have

about Jesus' public career is contained in three small books, any one of which can be read through in a half hour. On the face of it, the quest of the historical Jesus—if he is in these books—does not seem to be such a formidable undertaking. But perhaps that depends on where the quester starts from. As the local resident replied to the traveller seeking directions: *If I were going there, I wouldn't start from here!*

Schweitzer (22), summarizing the work of many Christian scholars who had laboured long on that quest, said of their results:

'The Jesus of Nazareth who came forward publicly as the Messiah, who preached the ethic of the Kingdom of God, who founded the Kingdom of heaven on earth, and died to give his work its final consecration, never had any existence. He is a figure designed by rationalism, endowed with life by liberalism, and clothed by modern theology in an historical garb.'

All research and not least that in the field of history requires that the seeker after truth have a certain attitude toward his work: There must be objectivity, freedom from preconceptions; respect for sources, and willingness to act upon any insight that comes to him regardless of where it leads. Thus one would do well to proceed here as might a visitor from Mars who knows nothing about Christianity or Jesus but does know how to use the historical method.

Recall that we are looking for an explanation of the *Jesus Phenomenon*. We want to account for the extraordinary person Jesus was. The conventional approach is to ask: *Why did Jesus live and die the way he did?* The conventional answer involves theological, speculative schematization, presupposing supernature, supermundane purpose, deity, magic, miracle. And that explanation carries with it the injunction: *You must believe!*

For at least 1800 years after Jesus' death, even quite sophisticated people were satisfied with a supernatural explanation of the *why* of Jesus' life and death. And even today, most Christians, regardless of their particular sect, accept such an explanation as a matter of course. This is so because Christians, like followers of other religions, depend on their priests for answers to their *why* questions in the same way that children depend on their parents. But there is this difference—the priest supplies the answers before the people ask the questions!

Gullibility can be a fatal disease. Clifford (17) warned: "It is wrong for anyone, anywhere, at any time to believe anything on insufficient evidence"—a statement with which every thinking person will agree.

A hundred years ago most people could accept a supernatural answer to the *why* question for that was the kind of Universe men supposed they were living in. But such answers are not so generally acceptable today. Intelligent, educated people know now that they are living in a world of Nature in which all living things evolved over a long period of time and, as old Heraclitus observed, everything is in a state of flux.

We also know that though Jesus lived about 2000 years ago, he was, in the perspective of human evolution, a contemporary of ours—physically identical—and though more intelligent than many of us, not at all different in kind. He was born as we were and grew up in a small village where everyone knew everyone else and thought of Jesus as just one of the local boys. He worked with his father at whatever carpenters did in those days. And then something happened to him on his way to the Jordan river. After that he wasn't the same. What was it that changed Jesus from the local boy every one knew to the man no one knew? *That is the question.*

About 400 years ago, Galileo changed Science by asking not *why* does a stone fall but *how* does it fall. And the mighty edifice of scientific knowledge has been slowly but securely erected on that foundation. It is high time that the same change was made in asking questions about religion.

The proper question is then: *How* did Jesus become the new person? By what process was he changed? If he changed himself, *How* did he do it?

The change in Jesus was quite astonishing to those who had known him before. Though he had a village background, he was able to stand up to the Scribes and Pharisees [20], charge them with hypocrisy and demonstrate their complete lack of any appreciation of what being religious really involved. And when his friends were alarmed at his temerity, he said: *Think ye that I came to cast peace on the earth? I tell you Nay, but rather division. For there shall be henceforth five in one house divided, three against two and two against three . . . And a man's foes shall be they of his own household. I came to cast fire upon the earth and what will I if it be already kindled?*

And that *fire*, kindled 2000 years ago has still not died out though every generation since and not least our own has found a way to avoid being burned by it. And should it blaze up again and seem likely to spread, how quickly will those who stoke it be swooped down upon by those others who fear that fire quite as much as did the religious leaders of Jesus' day—and for the same reason. And yet there was never a time when mankind had so great a need of that fire which Jesus cast upon the earth so long ago. Surely then, to learn HOW Jesus the carpenter from Nazareth became what he was is not only a worthwhile quest but an urgent necessity and an imperative task.

Arrived at the Jordan, Jesus attended a meeting at which his cousin John was preaching and calling upon people to repent and change their lives [19]. Many were responding to John's urging and were being baptised. The religious leaders scoffed at John and said that he was crazy. But Jesus accepted John's baptism, thus confirming his own repentance. And as he did so, Jesus had a profound psychological experience which he later described to others as hearing God say: *This day have I begotten thee* § 2.

This act of repentance—a conscious decision to change his life—resulted in Jesus having a sense that he had become God's man, subject to God.

God was now his King. He had entered the Kingdom of God. John did not bring this change about. God did not bring it about. Jesus himself brought it about. This is the HOW and the WHEN of the fundamental change in Jesus and this is the event which accounts for Jesus' subsequent activity—and for his striking ability to cope with all manner of people and situations. This is the secret of Jesus' remarkable life. What he did was not just another *New Year's Resolution*. It was something much more radical than that. It was a conscious decision, with no reservations, to set his life in a new direction. A commitment, *in advance*, to do God's Will—to do whatever he perceived to be *right* in each situation [25].

Following this experience, Jesus withdrew to be by himself while he thought about the meaning and significance of what had happened, § 3. Contemporary expectations were that God would send his Emissary, the Christ, to prepare for and actually establish the Kingdom of God [20, 23]. Reflecting on the meaning of his status as God's subject, Jesus considers his relationship to the current Messianic notions. He decides that the Political-leadership concept of Christ's role, involving war with Rome, is thoroughly evil. He will have nothing to do with that kind of activity. He will do only what is right. He will serve God alone.

Jesus sees the possibility that in doing God's will he may at some point find his life in danger. Can he expect God to rescue him? He decides not.

12 / THIS IS THE PROPHET JESUS

God will not intervene [24]. He decides that he must take full responsibility for his own actions and accept the consequences.

Jesus is aware of the economic plight of the Jewish people. But even if there were an abundance of food, he knows that a full belly is not the same as a full life. He will devote himself to helping people satisfy that more fundamental need.

Jesus returns to Nazareth and talks with people —presumably about his experience at the Jordan. We don't know what he said but from the reaction of his audience it is clear that what he said was new and authoritative—it must have come directly out of his own experience. People came in large numbers to hear him. The word soon got around. The religious leaders, guardians of the Law and ever zealous to see that it is kept, come to make sure that this lay-teacher does not get *out of line*. But he does. He says things that are unorthodox, radical, even subversive. He is leading the people astray, encouraging disrespect for the Law —and by implication, for the Lawyers, § 9. This won't do at all. The religious leaders consider how best to destroy Jesus, § 13.

Since people were expecting the Messiah (Christ) to appear at any time and since Jesus was a striking character whose presence was impressive and who spoke with authority, it began to be noised about that maybe he was the Christ. Some were even bold enough to address him as such. This brought an immediate denial from Jesus, § 6, 15. He was not the Christ, but he did admit to being a Prophet, § 26.

The religious leaders were critical and threatening, but worse, their conception of the Kingdom of God was wrong and they were apparently quite unaware of the social consequences of their outlook and practice. Jesus decides to confront them by comparing their standards with his own.

In the so-called *Sermon on the Mount*, § 17, Jesus shows that the religion of his critics is, to a great extent, mere mechanical rule-serving which is largely motivated by the desire to maintain a public-image as religious persons. Jesus' own religion is quite other—it consists in doing the Will of God—and doing it in secret. External codes such as Moses' commandments are not what religion is about—they have to do with the maintenance of viable social relations. Religion is about obedience to that inner guide—the Counsel of God—one's own conscience. [25].

Moses said that if you commit murder or adultery, your relationship with God will be broken. Jesus said that hate, lust, retaliation—evil thoughts—will break your relationship with God just as surely. It is one's emotional state that is determinative [22]. *To look on a woman to lust after her* was equivalent to adultery in its effect on one's awareness of the prompting of conscience. On the matter of oaths, Jesus pointed out that if you are honest there is no need to take an oath that you will tell the truth. Retaliation to avenge a wrong does not settle the matter, but forgiveness does. Religious practices such as alms giving, prayer and fasting, if done in public are done to gain public approval. To obtain God's approval, the sense that one is doing what is right for its own sake, righteous acts must be done in secret. Before one criticises others, one had better carry self-criticism to the limit. Paying tribute to Jesus will get you nowhere, but doing the Will of God will get you into the Kingdom of God. And finally, Jesus pointed out that if you wish to have satisfactory relationships with other people, you must treat them as you, yourself, would like to be treated. This calls for honesty.

The manner of the coming of the Kingdom of God was the theme of another discourse, § 24. At the time the Jews believed that the Kingdom of God was coming soon but there was controversy as to the manner of its coming [20]. Some believed that the Christ would come first and drive out the Romans and then God's Kingdom could be realized. Others believed that the Kingdom could not come until all the people were righteous and since many were not and were unlikely to become so, the role of the Christ was to judge, separate and eliminate the wicked. It was assumed, of course, that this Kingdom was for the Jews exclusively.

In his discourse on the coming of the Kingdom of God, Jesus undertook to correct many illusions held by the people. The most devastating revelation was that admission to the Kingdom of God was not a birthright of the Jews but was available to anyone who was willing to pay the admission fee. The cost—all that one has!

The motivation for paying such a high admission fee is however very strong for one obtains something of supreme value for oneself, namely, wholeness, fullness of life. Thus the motivation for entering the Kingdom of God is quite selfish. Nothing wrong with that. But the means is to become selfless. One must commit one's self *in advance*, without reservation, to do God's Will at all times. And what is God's Will? It is what one perceives to be Good, RIGHT. One is to obey one's conscience [25]. One volunteers to become the King's subject and thereafter one obeys the King in all things at all times.

This decision, consciously taken and resolutely followed, results in the integration of the personality. One becomes a whole person as a result of wanting just one thing and that a thing which is always available, namely, willingness to do God's Will. Fear, anxiety, insecurity disappear. As a whole person without the insecurity which was formerly such a distraction, one is able to cope with life's problems. Whatever personal assets one has—health, strength, sensitivity, imagination, intelligence—all become available for use— no inner conflict. Further, one is doing what one wants to be doing and so does it freely and joyously. This is Jesus' great discovery—his Way to Life. This is Jesus' conception of how the Kingdom of God will come about. And since it came that way for him, it could come in the same way for anyone else. It is experimental. Anyone may try it.

Thus the Kingdom of God would grow slowly

by individual increments—individuals making the decision to go THAT WAY. But note: in this concept *there is no role for the Christ.* There was no need to drive out the Romans for, as Jesus said, one must *Render unto Caesar the things that are Caesar's and unto God the things that are God's.* One could thus pay taxes to Rome without being disloyal to God. Further there was no need for a Christ to separate the good from the evil. Those who choose to make God (good) their King have their reward and the others *just go on stewing in their own ambivalence,* so to speak. The individual must make the choice which way he will go—a Broad Way which is easy but leads to emptiness or a Narrow Way which is hard but leads to fullness of Life. Not many, says Jesus, take the latter route.

So the Christ concept was the product of fantasy. It had been conceived to provide an agent, from God, who would perform tasks which were believed to be urgently necessary. Jesus found these tasks were quite unnecessary. One could pay taxes to Rome without being disloyal to God and one could be in the Kingdom of God even though most of one's contemporaries were not.

Obviously this understanding of the meaning of the Kingdom of God was so radical in relation to current conceptions that it would have been very dangerous for Jesus to explain it to his audience in plain speech. And yet it was of the greatest importance that people should know the truth about the matter for they were being led dangerously astray by the literal, simplistic notions of the religious leaders. On this theme, therefore, Jesus spoke in parables—he used simple stories, each with a central point or focus.

When Jesus was alone the disciples came to him and said unto him, Why speakest thou unto them in parables? And he said unto them, Unto you is given the mystery of the Kingdom of God: but unto them that are without, all things are done in parables: that seeing they may see, and not perceive; and hearing they may hear, and not understand. Give not that which is holy unto the dogs, neither cast your pearls before the swine, lest haply they trample them under their feet, and turn and rend you.

Jesus was concerned that his disciples should understand his conception of how the Kingdom of God would come, for the attitude of the religious leaders toward him being what it was, it could well be that he would be eliminated (as was John) and in that case, the future of his teaching would be up to the disciples.

To give his disciples some experience in carrying his message to the people, Jesus sent them out in twos with instructions concerning what to do and how to behave. It seems probable, however, that what they actually told people was that Jesus was the Christ. At any rate, when they returned, the crowds increased enormously, § 29. Soon thereafter, Jesus raised the question with his disciples: *Who say ye that I am?* And Peter, whether speaking for the group or only for himself, immediately blurted out, without hesitation; *Thou art the Christ*: § 33. Jesus at once told his disciples that he was not the Christ and that when he reached Jerusalem he would be rejected by the religious authorities and would probably be killed as had other prophets who had preceded him. To this deplorable prospect, Peter raised strong objection only to be castigated by Jesus and ordered: *Get thee behind me Satan; Thou mindest not the things of God but the things of men.*

Fully aware now that the disciples have associated themselves with him because of the potential of that association—assuming that he was the Christ—Jesus proceeds to lay down explicitly the conditions for discipleship: deny the self, lose the life. Here we come upon Jesus' *Paradox*—his statement of the way to a full and abundant life, § 35. *Whosoever would save his life shall lose it,* but, *Whosoever shall lose his life shall save it.* Of this saying, A. E. Housman, Poet, Classical Scholar and Fellow of Trinity College, Cambridge, said: *This is the most important truth ever uttered and the greatest discovery ever made.*

It is a saying that is difficult to understand but worth struggling with.

Jesus now set his face toward Jerusalem which he would reach in time for the Passover celebration. He teaches along the way but his mood is sombre. This he knows is probably a death-walk for him but there is still work to be done. As each situation arises he deals with it—teaching now about tolerance—then about efficacious prayer, forgiveness, the way to greatness, ideal marriage and the question of divorce. He directs attention to the *signs-of-the-times*, the activity of some young Jewish dissidents to Roman rule. He cites the case of some young Galileans *whose blood Pilate had mingled with their sacrifices.* These attacks were made by members of a revolutionary party, the Zealots, based in Galilee. They rejected any form of collaboration with the Romans and refused to pay taxes on religious grounds. They had some supporters among the Pharisees and other influential people. The national expectation of a Messiah (Christ) coming as a liberator, played a considerable role in motivating those in the revolutionary movement [21].

At last Jerusalem is reached. As he enters with his followers, he is acclaimed as *The Prophet Jesus from Nazareth of Galilee.* Jesus teaches daily in the Temple. He attacks the religious leaders who try to catch him with trick questions. It is important to those leaders that they succeed in getting Jesus into the hands of the Roman Governor for if Pilate can be persuaded that Jesus is a political liability to the regime, he will be disposed of without further risk to them.

As the attacks by the Zealots increased and the Roman reaction became quite ruthless, it was clear to Jesus that unless there came a fundamental change in the outlook of these freedom-fighters and their supporters, the situation must lead to an all-out war. And that was a further reason for the continued teaching of his version of how the Kingdom of God was to come about. For if that were well understood then the conception which required that the Romans be driven out would be undermined and discredited. Obviously the Romans were in Palestine to make a profit and they could not be expected to just go on indefinitely letting themselves be pushed around by a few stubborn, fanatical young Jews. Eventually, Jerusalem would be attacked, § 82 [21] (19).

In anticipation of this catastrophe, which Jesus supposed would come soon, and concerned lest his disciples, who must carry on his message, become its victims, he tells them: If you are in Judea when the attack on Jerusalem comes, flee to the mountains. And if you are in Jerusalem, leave at once. For these will be days of vengeance.

Jesus imagines what will happen. There will be a panic situation. People will call on God to send the Messiah to save them. There will be a tendency to stop work and look to the Heavens for an intervention. But Jesus knows there will be no intervention, § 3. How is he to get the expectation of an intervention out of the minds of his disciples? Answer—change the scenario. Introduce a new (though ancient) character—THE SON OF MAN —having a function which is quite unrelated to the crisis situation. See [20] end.

He tells the disciples: *The days will come when ye shall desire to see the Day of the Son of Man and ye shall not see it. And they shall say to you, Lo, There! Lo, Here! Go not away nor follow after them. Take heed that no man lead you astray. For many shall come, saying, I am the Christ; and, The Time is at hand. They shall lead many astray. Go not after them. For as the lightning . . . so shall the SON OF MAN be in his day.* He tells them: You hope God will intervene and he will indeed. He will send his agent The Son of Man. But the Son of Man will not save you from the Romans. He will come as a judge of men and to assign to each a destiny appropriate to his essential nature. Since he will come *as the lightning*, there will be no point in standing around *watching* for his arrival. There is no way to anticipate where lightning will strike. And there will be no point in *waiting* for it either, for the Coming is not imminent. Only God knows when it will happen. And there is no way to anticipate the outcome—one will be taken and another will be left. There is nothing anyone can do about *THAT*. But there is something all of you *can* do and that is *TEACH*. I have taught you all that you were capable of learning about the Kingdom of God. Now you have an obligation and a responsibility to pass on to others what I have taught you about how God's Kingdom will come.

Behold I send you forth as sheep in the midst of wolves. Be ye therefore wise as serpents and harmless as doves. Take heed to yourselves: for they shall deliver you up to Councils; and in Synagogues shall ye be beaten; and before Governors and Kings shall ye stand. And when they lead you to judgment, and deliver you up, be not anxious before hand what ye shall say; but whatever shall be given you in that hour, that speak ye. For it is not ye that speak but the Spirit of your Father that speaketh in you.

In the past Jesus had told them secretly about the Kingdom but the time had come now to speak openly. *There is nothing covered up that shall not be revealed and hid that shall not be known. What I tell you in the darkness, speak in the light and what ye hear in the ear, proclaim upon the housetops. . . . And I say unto you my friends be not afraid of them that kill the body and after that have no more that they can do.*

Thus did Jesus try to prepare his disciples for the war conditions which he believed would obtain sometime in the near future.

And now we come to the final act in this tragic drama. The religious authorities arrest Jesus at night and take him before a religious court where he is tried and, of course, found guilty. An effort is made to get Jesus to admit that he is the Christ for such an admission would be useful when they take him before the Governor. Jesus denies that he is the Christ but they take him to Pilate anyway and there charge him with claiming to be the Christ, a King and with stirring up the people and encouraging insurrection. Pilate does not believe what the religious leaders say nor does Herod who was in Jerusalem for the Passover feast and was called in by Pilate for an opinion. Having found no (political) fault in Jesus, Pilate was about to turn him loose. However, the religious leaders are vehement in their accusations and demand that Jesus be punished. So Pilate, in the interest of peace-at-any-price and purely as a matter of political expediency, orders Jesus' execution.

Now Jesus was dead. His disciples ran away afraid, frustrated, disillusioned. They had been certain that Jesus was the Christ and that he would reveal himself as such when they reached

Jerusalem. But it did not happen. For a time they were deeply depressed. "Then there came a whisper among them and stories, rather discrepant stories, that the body of Jesus was not in the tomb where it had been placed. And then one and then another had seen him alive. Soon they were consoling themselves with the conviction that he had risen from the dead, that he had shown himself to many and had ascended visibly into heaven. Witnesses were found to declare that they had positively seen him go up—through the blue—to God. Before long they had convinced themselves that he would come back to them again in a little while and in this bright revival of their old-time dream of a temporal-ruler they forgot the message, the revolutionary conception he had given them of the Kingdom of God." (36).

There was thus a shift in the minds of the disciples from the conception of a political Christ to an apocalyptic-eschatalogical Christ who would come soon on the *clouds of heaven in glory* to function as a judge of righteousness [23]. This belief held by Jesus' followers after his death became the basis for the establishment of the primitive church.

Christianity which grew from this early beginning was thus a religion about Jesus based on the assumption that he was the Christ of Jewish tradition.

While this was clearly a case of mistaken identity, it was perhaps inevitable in the circumstances. And since this belief that Jesus was the Christ was the foundation on which the Church was built, there was no way the later structure could possibly repudiate it. Nor was there any felt need or seen necessity to do so. On the contrary, early Christian scholars and Fathers of the Church laboured to strengthen that foundation by every conceivable means. And as the institution grew and became more powerful, its rationale as developed by its apologists reached the point where the truth about the historical Jesus was no longer of any importance to it. The Jesus of History and the Jesus of the Church came to have little in common save the name.

By asking HOW did Jesus become the remarkable person he was we have found an answer that involved neither magic nor miracle nor supernatural intervention. Rather what was involved was entirely human—the human will. Jesus *decided* to open himself completely to God—to express God's Will—whatever came to him as GOOD, the RIGHT thing to do in each situation. That is how Jesus entered the Kingdom of God and became a whole person. Anyone else may do the same. Granted it is not easy to shift from being totally self-willed to being totally GOOD-WILLED, yet that is the only alternative we have.

If one is interested in fullness of Life; freedom from fear, anxiety, insecurity; freedom from dependence upon all manner of external props—and who isn't? then it is time to try Jesus' religion. That is what it did for him and he invited others— you and me—to join him in the Kingdom of God.

* *

HOW THE GOSPEL MATERIAL FOR THIS STUDY WAS SELECTED

Much of the textural material for this book has been taken from the text of the late H. B. Sharman's *Jesus as Teacher.* In the introduction to that work, Dr. Sharman explained the basis of his selection of material from the synoptic accounts of the life of Jesus as follows (4):

"While it is highly instructive to work through the Records of the Life of Jesus and endeavour, through the use of the best methods of literary and historical criticism, to penetrate the layers of accretion and distortion which over the years, gathered about the person of Jesus, his public appearances and his teaching, that is properly a task for scholars or for a group of university graduates with the time and interest for such an adventure. Since our interest is limited to an examination of his teaching in the hope that we may discover the secret of his remarkable life, we shall have to be content with selections from the reports of his brief public career.

"In making these selections, the effort has been made to present most of the actual teaching material reported in Matthew, Luke and Mark. Sometimes the narrative material has been taken from one of the accounts; sometimes from another. The method has been to examine all of the material and to establish as far as this is possible, which of the three accounts has the greater historical probability. When this method fails, and it frequently does, then the selection is based on the personal opinion of the author as to what in his experience appears consistent with the general outlook of Jesus as this has been seen in large numbers of student groups where the more extensive study of the total body of material composing the narrative accounts has been made."

PART I

JESUS THE TEACHER

CHAPTER 1

ACTIVITY OF JOHN AND ITS RELATION TO JESUS

§ 1 Statement of the work of John.

In the fifteenth year of the reign of the Roman Emperor Tiberius, (about AD 27), when Pontius Pilate was Governor of Judea and Herod the Tetrarch of Galilee, John the son of Zacharias, a priest, and his cousin Jesus, son of Joseph, a carpenter, were each about thirty years of age.
It was at that time that:

the word of God came unto John
in the wilderness of Judæa. And he came into all the region round about Jordan, preaching the baptism of repentance unto remission of sins.
⁋Now John himself had his raiment of camel's hair, and a leathern girdle about his loins; and his food was locusts and wild honey.
Then went out unto him all they of Jerusalem, and all the country of Judæa, and all the region round about Jordan; and they were baptized of him in the river Jordan, confessing their sins.
⁋But when John saw many of the Pharisees and Sadducees coming to his baptism, he said unto them, Ye offspring of vipers, who warned you to flee from the wrath to come? Bring forth therefore fruits worthy

of repentance, and begin not to say within yourselves, We have Abraham to our father: for I say unto you, that God is able of these stones to raise up children unto Abraham. And even now is the axe also laid unto the root of the trees: every tree therefore that bringeth not forth good fruit is hewn down, and cast into the fire.

¶ And all the people when they heard, and the publicans, justified God, being baptized with the baptism of John. But the Pharisees and the lawyers rejected for themselves the counsel of God, being not baptized of him.

¶ And the multitudes asked John, saying, What then must we do? And he answered and said unto them, He that hath two coats, let him impart to him that hath none; and he that hath food, let him do likewise.

And there came also publicans to be baptized, and they said unto him, Teacher, what must we do? And he said unto them, Extort no more than that which is appointed you.

And soldiers also asked him, saying, And we, what must we do? And he said unto them, Do violence to no man, neither exact anything wrongfully; and be content with your wages.

¶ And as the people were in expectation, and all men reasoned in their hearts concerning John, whether haply he were the Christ; John answered, saying unto them all,

I indeed baptize you with water; but there cometh he that is mightier than I, the latchet of whose shoes I am not worthy to unloose: he shall baptize you with fire: whose fan is in his hand, throughly to cleanse his threshing-floor, and to gather the wheat into his garner; but the chaff he will burn up with unquenchable fire.

¶ With many other exhortations therefore preached John good tidings unto the people; but Herod the tetrarch, being reproved by him for Herodias his brother's wife, and for all the evil things which Herod had done, added yet this above all, that he shut up John in prison.

Whatever may have been the content of *the word* or its actual source, the experience provided John with a strong sense of mission—the need to urge people to repent of their sins. John was apparently convinced that the arrival of the long-awaited Messiah (Christ) was imminent and that on his coming—as judge of righteousness—there would be a separation of the good from the evil with destruction of the latter. Hence the urgent need for repentence [20, 23].

However, not everyone held this view of the future and the Messianic activity. The Pharisees, probably largely middle-class, believed that the Messiah would not come until the Jews were a righteous people. That condition met, the Messiah would establish the Kingdom of God. The Kingdom would of course be for Jews only.

It should be noted that there were some Pharisees who held a political-leadership function for the Messiah and ascribed to him the task of driving out the Romans. More of that later [21].

In reply to those who having been baptised,

sought guidance concerning the *fruits of repentance* which they ought now to bring forth, John prescribed ethical behaviour, honesty, sharing with others, non-violence. John was a strong striking character and it was natural that, under the circumstances—*people were in expectation*—there would be the suspicion that he, himself, was the Christ. John not only denied any such distinction but there is no evidence here that he thought Jesus was that personage either. See § 19.

§2 Baptism of Jesus by John

Now it came to pass, when all the people were baptized of John in the Jordan, that, Jesus also having been baptized, and praying, the heaven was opened, and the Spirit of God descended, as a dove, upon him. And a voice came out of heaven: Thou art my beloved Son; this day have I begotten thee.

Assuming that Jesus was an honest, sincere young man of better than average intelligence, who was steeped in the religious history of his people and hence aware of the hopes and expectations of his contemporaries, it would be natural that he would be intrigued by the reports of John's activity.

On seeing John and hearing him speak, Jesus must have been impressed by the man's sincerity and call to righteousness, and was challenged to repent just as were other people present. And since we have assumed that he was honest, we must suppose that Jesus would not have accepted John's baptism as a symbol of repentance unless he had indeed repented—resolved to change his life.

Whatever it was that Jesus actually did (cause), he immediately had a profound psychological experience (effect). Rightly or wrongly, he had a sense that he had, by his act, become God's man. God had *begotten him*—not a part of him, but all of him then, on that day.

This subjective experience was not due to something that God did nor to something that John did. It resulted from something that Jesus himself did. *N. B. All of Jesus' subsequent activity flows from this event—the decision he made at that time.*

NOTE ON BIBLICAL TEXT

Concerning Jesus' baptismal experience, the English Revised Version (ERV 1881), reads:
Mark 1:11—*Thou art my beloved son, in Thee I am well pleased.*
Luke 3:22—Copies Mark exactly.
Matthew 3:17—*This is my beloved son in whom I am well pleased.*
Thus the report in Mark and hence in Luke is subjective; that in Matthew is objective—an announcement which could have been heard by others.

In the Jerusalem Bible (JB), 1966 (5) Luke reads, concerning this event, *You are my son, the beloved. My favour rests on you.*

In the New English Bible (NEB), New Testament, Second Edition, 1970 (6), Luke reads: *Thou art my son, the beloved, on thee my favour rests.*

In each book, (JB) and (NEB), there is a foot-note referring to this event which says: "Some witnesses (sources) read:

(JB) *You are my son—today I have become your father.*

(NEB) *My son art thou, this day I have begotten thee.*

Sharman's *Jesus as Teacher*, 1935 (4) which is followed here, reads:

Thou art my beloved son; this day have I begotten thee.

The difference between the wordings chosen by (JB) and (NEB) scholars for inclusion in their texts and the footnote which each group attached but did not use, is fundamental.

§3   Withdrawal of Jesus to the Wilderness

And Jesus, full of the Spirit of God, returned from the Jordan, and was led by the Spirit in the wilderness during forty days, being tempted of the devil.

¶And he led Jesus up, and shewed him all the kingdoms of the world in a moment of time. And the devil said unto him, To thee will I give all this authority, and the glory of them: if thou wilt worship before me, it shall all be thine. And Jesus answered and said unto him, It is written, Thou shalt worship the Lord thy God, and him only shalt thou serve.

¶And he led Jesus to Jerusalem, and set him on the pinnacle of the temple, and said unto him, If thou art the Son of God, cast thyself down from hence: for it is written,

   He shall give his angels charge concerning thee,
      to guard thee:

And on their hands they shall bear thee up,
Lest haply thou dash thy foot against a stone.
And Jesus answering said unto him, It is said, Thou shalt not tempt the Lord thy God.
¶ And the devil said unto Jesus, If thou art the Son of God, command this stone that it become bread. And Jesus answered unto him, It is written, Man shall not live by bread alone.

It is surely no surprise that after this profound experience Jesus decided to get away by himself for a while to consider the meaning and practical implications of his new status. If he is in fact God's subject, then God is his King and, for him, the Kingdom of God has come—and without the coming of the Christ—unless indeed he is that person.

Here we find Jesus examining contemporary forms of leadership. The question of his personal relationship to direct political rule is a vital issue because of the current political situation. Some of the religious leaders and others expected God to send a political leader, the Christ, who would make war on the enemies of the Jews [21] [23, first part].

After examining the implications of this political concept Jesus saw what would be involved for himself personally in accepting that role and rejected it as being evil. He would serve God; he would do only what was good.

The suggestion that he could choose a public career that would expose him to great physical hazard and expect to escape the consequences of his acts—that because of his special status, God would intervene to save him, is also rejected by Jesus as an evil suggestion. Jesus became God's subject by his own act, not as a result of some intervention by God. So, he is on his own.

Finally there is the stones-to-bread episode—so many stones, so little bread. A seemingly easy solution to the problem of the poverty of his people. However, this also would involve supernatural intervention and he has already rejected that as something available to him. And even if the economic problem were solved, Jesus knows that a full belly is not the same as a full life—a fact that we moderns are beginnning to rediscover rather belatedly.

If thou art the Son of God (Christ) . . .

Jesus has here considered and evaluated the various contemporary forms of the role of the Christ and rejected them all as essentially wrong. Not only is he not the Christ, but the concept itself is evil.

One may wonder why Jesus had not set about evaluating these Christly concepts earlier. Perhaps he had, but obviously it was not a personal problem earlier. However his new insight into the meaning of the Kingship of God has given him a new perspective and forced upon him the task of evaluating the Christ concept itself.

Jesus knows that he has become God's man— God is his King and this has come about as a result of his own choice and decision. *This is the important thing to grasp.*

What will Jesus do now? For a start he could tell people about his experience at the Jordan—what he did and what the result was—a cause-effect relationship, open to experiment. He could urge others to do what he had done. But dare he tell them the various concepts of the role of the Christ are wrong and that the Kingdom of God does not come that way? See § 24.

CHAPTER 2

Beginnings of the Public Activity of Jesus

§4   Jesus Teaches at Nazarêth

And Jesus came to Nazarêth, where he had been brought up: and he entered, as his cuŝtom was, into the synagogue on the sabbath day, and ŝtood up to read. And there was delivered unto him the book of the prophêt Isaiah. And he opened the book, and found the place where it was written,
   The Spirit of the Lord is upon me,
   Because he anointed me to preach good tidings to
      the poor:
   He hath sent me to proclaim release to the captives,
   To sêt at liberty them that are bruised,
   To proclaim the acceptable year of the Lord.
And he closed the book, and gave it back to the attendant, and sat down. And the eyes of all in the synagogue were faŝtened on him. And all bare him witness, and wondered at the words of grace which proceeded out of his mouth.
And they said, Is not this Joseph's son?
Jesus himself, when he began to teach, was about thirty years of age, being the son (as was supposed) of Joseph.

That sense of prophetic mission which possessed Isaiah made it altogether natural that he should speak as reported in the portion of the scripture which Jesus elected to read on this occasion. Isaiah's encouraging words had of course had practical fulfillment many centuries before Jesus' time in the return of the Jews from the Babylonian captivity. Evidently Jesus' own recent experience made him feel that this classical expression of the prophetic consciousness would be an appropriate setting for his own message to the people of his own home town. The question *Is not this Joseph's son?* suggests that, in the past, the people of Nazareth had not known Jesus as being strikingly different from the other local boys.

§5   Jesus Teaches at Capernaum

And Jesus came down to Capernaum, a city of Galilee. And straightway on the sabbath day he entered into the synagogue and taught. And they were astonished at his teaching: for he taught them as having authority, and not as the scribes.
And they were all amazed, insomuch that they questioned among themselves, saying, What is this? a new teaching!
And the report of him went out straightway everywhere into all the region of Galilee round about.

The authority for the Scribes was the Scripture. They quoted from the Law and the Prophets. Jesus' authority was his own firsthand experience.

He had gained new insight. It was indeed a new teaching.

§6 Jesus and Mental Cases

And straightway, when Jesus was come out of the synagogue, he came into the house. And at even, when the sun did set, they brought unto Jesus them that were possessed with devils. And all the city was gathered together at the door. And he cast out many devils. And the devils came out crying and saying,
Ah! What have we to do with thee, thou Jesus of Nazareth, thou Son of the Most High God? Art thou come to torment us? Art thou come to destroy us? We know thee who thou art, the Holy One of God! And rebuking them, Jesus suffered them not to speak, because they believed that he was the Christ.

Whatever may have been the source of their information, these disturbed people evidently believed that Jesus was the Christ [20]. Perhaps they were saying aloud what others were hinting and whispering. Jesus *suffered them not to speak* because he knew he was not the personage they had in mind and he wished to stop that rumour before it went any further.

§7 Jesus Wins Fisherman Followers

Now it came to pass, while the multitude pressed upon Jesus and heard the word of God, that he was standing by the lake of Gennesaret.
And he saw two boats standing by the lake: but the

BEGINNINGS OF THE PUBLIC ACTIVITY OF JESUS / 41

fishermen had gone out of them, and were washing their nets. And he entered into one of the boats, which was Simon's, and asked him to put out a little from the land. And he sat down and taught the multitudes out of the boat. And when Jesus had left speaking, he said unto Simon, Put out into the deep, and let down your nets for a draught. And Simon answered and said, Master, we toiled all night, and took nothing: but at thy word I will let down the nets. And when they had this done, they inclosed a great multitude of fishes. And they beckoned unto their partners in the other boat, that they should come and help them. And they came, and filled both the boats. And Simon was amazed at the draught of the fishes which they had taken; and so were also James and John, sons of Zebedee, which were partners with Simon. But Simon Peter fell down at Jesus' knees, saying, Depart from me; for I am a sinful man, O Master. And Jesus said unto Simon, Fear not; from henceforth thou shalt catch men. And when they had brought their boats to land, they left all, and followed Jesus.

Jesus taught from the boat because the multitude *pressed upon Him.* He remained in the boat instead of landing after he had finished speaking for the same reason.

Peter was evidently impressed by the person of

Jesus. His reaction was not unlike that of the disturbed people in § 6. Jesus may have been talking about repentance. He invited Peter to join him in *catching men.* Such was his conception of his work.

§8 Jesus Teaches Throughout Galilee

And in the morning, a great while before day, Jesus rose up and went out, and departed into a desert place, and there prayed.
And Simon and they that were with him followed after him; and they found him, and say unto him, All are seeking thee.
And Jesus saith unto them, Let us go elsewhere into the next towns, that I may preach there also; for to this end came I forth.
And he went into their synagogues throughout all Galilee teaching.

Jesus had a message to deliver, § 4, but an unexpected development, § 6, began to interfere with his chosen activity. So he went off by himself for a period of prayer—seeking insight—what is the right thing for me to do now? Peter and the others are eager for the crowds, but Jesus is single-minded. He must tell his story to as many different people as possible. What was his story?

CHAPTER 3

Development of Opposition to Jesus

§9 Criticism of Free Forgiveness for Sin.

AND when Jesus entered again into Capernaum after some days, it was noised that he was in the house. And many were gathered together, so that there was no longer room for them, no, not even about the door.
And Jesus was teaching. And there were Pharisees and doctors of the law sitting by, which were come out of every village of Galilee and Judæa and Jerusalem.
And behold, men bring on a bed a man that was palsied: and they sought to bring him in, and to lay him before Jesus. And not finding by what way they might bring him in because of the multitude, they went up to the housetop, and let him down through the tiles with his couch into the midst before Jesus.
And Jesus seeing their faith saith unto the sick of the palsy, Son, thy sins are forgiven. But there were certain of the scribes sitting there, and reasoning in their hearts, Why doth this man thus speak? he blasphemeth: who can forgive sins but one, even God?
And straightway Jesus, perceiving in his spirit that they so reasoned within themselves, saith unto them, Why reason ye these things in your hearts? Man hath authority on earth to forgive sins.

Then Jesus saith to the sick of the palsy, I say unto thee, Arise, take up thy bed, and go unto thy house. And he arose, and departed to his house. But when the multitudes saw it, they glorified God, which had given such authority unto men.

This is the first reference to the presence of Scribes and Pharisees in Jesus' audience [20]. Again the demand for healing interferes with the teaching mission. It may have been a current notion that illness was a result of sin.

According to the tenets of orthodox Judaism, the Scribes were quite right in their criticism. Sin was by definition a failure to obey the Law—an offence against God. Only God could forgive the offence and he would do so only at a price. The sinner must repent and present a suitable sacrificial offering in the Temple [20]. Unfortunately, the complexities of the Law as detailed by the Scribes were such that the common people found it a great burden and deviations from it difficult to avoid.

Here, people bring a palsied man believing the rumour that Jesus was the Christ—from God. Surely God's agent would help their friend. Jesus, *seeing their faith*, (for faith read confidence in God), simply stated that the man's sins were forgiven. The Scribes understood that Jesus was himself forgiving the man's sins which, from their point of view, would of course be blasphemy.

Jesus evidently had the insight that God was not involved in any way in forgiveness. What was involved was the attitude of the sinner. And so,

Jesus could say, as could any perceptive man, *Thy sins are forgiven.* See also § 20.

The religious Establishment thought otherwise. It had a system, a formula, dating back centuries which, being inflexible, had no room for a new conception of sin and still less for a new conception of man's possible relationship to God.

This matter of sin and forgiveness bears thinking about. What actually goes on psychologically within the person when he sins? Against whom or what does he sin? What is it that is denied or ignored, leaving a sense of guilt? [19, 25].

§10 Criticism for Association with Sinners

And Jesus went forth again by the sea side; and all the multitude resorted unto him, and he taught them.
And as Jesus passed by, he saw Levi the son of Alphæus sitting at the place of toll, and he saith unto him, Follow me. And he arose and followed him. And it came to pass, that he was sitting at meat in his house, and many publicans and sinners sat down with Jesus and his disciples: for there were many, and they followed him.
And the scribes of the Pharisees, when they saw that Jesus was eating with the sinners and publicans, said unto his disciples, He eatêth and drinkêth with publicans and sinners. And when Jesus heard it, he saith unto them,
They that are whole have no need of a physician, but they that are sick: I came not to call the righteous, but sinners.
But go ye and learn what this meanêth, I desire mercy, and not sacrifice.

In his baptismal experience Jesus had the sense that God had that day *begotten him.* Subsequently he had devoted himself to teaching. Prior to his baptism he evidently regarded himself as a sinner and on that occasion he decided to let God (good) control his life. He became *God's man.*

Here Jesus is associating with people who are as he was. No doubt he felt more at home with the common people—he was one of them. But he says that they are sick and he is a physician. His vocation as he saw it was to provide a cure for the sickness of the people so they might become whole as he himself had. Religion for Jesus had a healing function.

I desire mercy and not sacrifice. In this quotation from the prophet Hosea, Jesus is saying that in their rigid adherence to formal, mechanical practices, his critics have blinded themselves to the real need of the sinner. In Hosea's thought, mercy—that is help, non-rejection of the sinner—was the only useful procedure.

§11 Criticism of Attitude toward Fasting

And John's disciples and the Pharisees were fasting: and they come and say unto Jesus, Why do John's disciples and the disciples of the Pharisees fast, but thy disciples fast not?
And Jesus said unto them, Can the sons of the bridechamber fast, while the bridegroom is with them? as long as they have the bridegroom with them, they cannot fast. But when the bridegroom shall be taken away from them, then will they fast.

Jesus was an original thinker; he always went back to the origin of any practice to ask what was there at the beginning. Out of what human situation or condition did this, now arbitrary and mechanical practice of fasting, develop? His answer is: feasting goes with rejoicing; fasting goes with affliction. These are normal human reactions. The use of the word *bridegroom* simply sets the scene—a joyous event. It has no personal reference.

§12 Criticism for Working on the Sabbath

And it came to pass, that Jesus was going on the sabbath day through the cornfields; and his disciples began, as they went, to pluck the ears of corn. And the Pharisees said unto him, Behold, why do they on the sabbath day that which is not lawful?
And Jesus said unto them, Did ye never read what David did, when he had need, and was an hungred, he, and they that were with him? How he entered into the house of God, and did eat the shewbread, which it is not lawful to eat save for the priests, and gave also to them that were with him?
Or have ye not read in the law, how that on the sabbath day the priests in the temple profane the sabbath, and are guiltless?
And Jesus said unto them, The sabbath was made for man, and not man for the sabbath: so that man is lord even of the sabbath.

The original commandment *Remember the Sabbath day to keep it holy*, had become, under

Scribal influence, a monstrous thing with a multitude of detailed prohibitions. Here the Pharisees found Jesus' disciples guilty, for they *plucked the ears of corn* which is *harvesting* and forbidden on the Sabbath.

Jesus cites two precedents which his critics can scarcely ignore: King David, when hungry, disregarded the Law and encouraged others to do so. Further, the priests in the temple also broke the Law when they required food.

Jesus concludes that man's need determines what he may do on the Sabbath. It is man himself, knowing his needs, who must decide what is appropriate for him to do on that day.

§13 Culmination of Criticism of Jesus

And the Pharisees went out, and straightway with the Herodians took counsel against Jesus, how they might destroy him.

Jesus has now been criticized by the religious leaders on four points—forgiveness of sins; association with sinners, attitude toward fasting and sabbath observance. The most serious of these departures from their norm was the first—as indeed it still is in our own day.

Jesus' attitude toward the Law, as revealed in these four episodes made it inevitable that he would be regarded by the religious leaders as a dangerous radical, out to destroy religion and subvert the common people. And the favourable response of the people to him—less, it would seem, for his teaching than from the belief that he was the Christ—appeared to call for immediate corrective action, by the guardians of the Law.

At the time, Herod was the Roman Tetrarch of Galilee. The *Herodians* were those who were *in* with Herod. Only the Roman rulers could make life and death decisions.

§14 Attitude of Jesus Toward Criticism

And Jesus spake also parables unto them:
No man rendeth a piece from a new garment and putteth it upon an old garment; else he will rend the new, and also the piece from the new will not agree with the old.
And no man putteth new wine into old wine-skins; else the new wine will burst the skins, and itself will be spilled, and the skins will perish. But new wine must be put into fresh wine-skins.
And no man having drunk old wine desireth new: for he saith, The old is good.

A parable is a story with a central, focal point; the details are not separately significant. *The point here is* that Jesus had something new to say and it would be inappropriate or impossible to say it in the old form. He evidently did not expect those who were profitably attached to the conventional wisdom to appreciate his teaching.

CHAPTER 4

Definition of Standards of Righteousness by Jesus

§15 Widespread Fame of Jesus

AND Jesus with his disciples withdrew to the sea: and a great multitude from Galilee followed. And from Judæa, and from Jerusalem, and from Idumæa, and beyond Jordan, and about Tyre and Sidon, a great multitude, hearing what great things he did, came unto him.

And he spake to his disciples, that a little boat should wait on him because of the crowd, lest they should throng him: for as many as had plagues pressed upon him that they might touch him.

And the unclean spirits, whensoever they beheld him, fell down before him, and cried, saying, Thou art the Son of God. And he charged them much that they should not make him known.

Here again we find Jesus resorting to the use of a boat so that he might not be overwhelmed by the crowd or prevented from speaking by the insistent demands of the physically and mentally handicapped people who were present. These latter were present apparently because they, or those who were with them believed, mistakenly, that

Jesus was the Christ. Again he tries, urgently, to correct them.

§16 Appointment of Twelve Associates

And it came to pass in these days, that Jesus went out into the mountain to pray; and he continued all night in prayer to God. And when it was day, he called his disciples: and he chose from them twelve, that they might be with him, and that he might send them forth: Simon, whom he also named Peter, and Andrew his brother; and James the son of Zebedee, and John the brother of James; and Philip and Bartholomew; and Matthew and Thomas; and James the son of Alphæus, and Simon which was called the Zealot; and Judas the son of James, and Judas Iscariot, which was the traitor.

As in § 8, Jesus withdraws to pray, § 47. The multitude of people and especially the sick whose interest apparently depends on their identification of him with the Christ, have created a problem. And even more important perhaps is the unrelenting criticism of the religious leaders which he takes seriously.

The people must be warned against the ominous outlook of the Scribes and Pharisees. The attitude of those leaders toward him suggests that he may be prevented from continuing his teaching mission. What to do? Perhaps the thing to do is to select some followers as associates; give them special training—*an immersion course*, and send them out with the message. Then if he is removed from the scene as John was, his associates will be able to carry on.

§17 Discourse on Standards of Righteousness

And Jesus came down with the twelve, and stood on a level place. And a great multitude of his disciples, and a great number of the people from all Judæa and Jerusalem, and the sea coast of Tyre and Sidon, came to hear him.
¶ And Jesus lifted up his eyes on his disciples, and said: Blessed are ye poor.
Blessed are ye that hunger.
Blessed are ye that weep.
Blessed are ye when men persecute you.
Ye are the salt of the earth.
Ye are the light of the world.
¶ Think not that I came to destroy the law or the prophets: I came not to destroy, but to fulfil. For I say unto you, that except your righteousness shall exceed the righteousness of the scribes and Pharisees, ye shall in no wise enter into the kingdom of God.
¶ Ye have heard that it was said to them of old time, Thou shalt not kill; and whosoever shall kill shall be in danger of the judgement: but I say unto you, that every one who is angry with his brother shall be in danger of the judgement.
If therefore thou art offering thy gift at the altar, and there rememberest that thy brother hath aught against thee, leave there thy gift before the altar, and go thy way, first be reconciled to thy brother, and then come and offer thy gift.

Blessed are the peacemakers: for they shall be called sons of God.

⁋ Ye have heard that it was said, Thou shalt not commit adultery: but I say unto you, that every one that looketh on a woman to lust after her hath committed adultery with her already in his heart. And if thine eye causeth thee to stumble, pluck it out, and cast it from thee: for it is profitable for thee that one of thy members should perish, and not thy whole body. And if thy hand causeth thee to stumble, cut it off, and cast it from thee: for it is profitable for thee that one of thy members should perish, and not thy whole body.

Blessed are the pure in heart: for they shall see God.

⁋ Again, ye have heard that it was said to them of old time, Thou shalt not forswear thyself, but shalt perform unto the Lord thine oaths: but I say unto you, Swear not at all; neither by the heaven, nor by the earth, nor by Jerusalem. Neither shalt thou swear by thy head. But let your speech be, Yea, yea; Nay, nay: and whatsoever is more than these is of evil.

⁋ Ye have heard that it was said, An eye for an eye, and a tooth for a tooth: but I say unto you, Resist not evil: but whosoever smiteth thee on thy right cheek, turn to him the other also. And if any man would take away thy cloke, let him have thy coat also. And whosoever shall compel thee to go one mile, go with him twain.

Blessed are the meek: for they shall inherit the earth.

⁋ Ye have heard that it was said, Thou shalt love thy neighbour, and hate thine enemy: but I say unto you, Love your enemies, do good to them that hate you, bless them that curse you, pray for them that despitefully use you.

If ye love them that love you, what thank have ye? for even sinners love those that love them. And if ye do good to them that do good to you, what thank have ye? for even sinners do the same.

Ye shall be sons of the Most High: for he is kind toward the unthankful and evil: he maketh his sun to rise on the evil and the good, and sendeth rain on the just and the unjust. Be ye merciful, even as your Father is merciful.

Blessed are the merciful: for they shall obtain mercy.

¶ Take heed that ye do not your righteousness before men, to be seen of them: else ye have no reward with your Father.

¶ When therefore thou doest alms, sound not a trumpet before thee, as the hypocrites do in the synagogues and in the streets, that they may have glory of men. Verily I say unto you, They have received their reward. But when thou doest alms, let not thy left hand know what thy right hand doeth: that thine alms may be in secret: and thy Father which seeth in secret shall recompense thee.

¶ And when ye pray, ye shall not be as the hypocrites: for they love to stand and pray in the synagogues and in the corners of the streets, that they may be seen of men. Verily I say unto you, They have received their reward. But thou, when thou prayest, enter into thine inner chamber, and having shut thy door, pray to thy Father which is in secret, and thy Father which seeth in secret shall recompense thee.

¶ Moreover when ye fast, be not, as the hypocrites, of a sad countenance: for they disfigure their faces, that they may be seen of men to fast. Verily I say unto you,

They have received their reward. But thou, when thou fastest, anoint thy head, and wash thy face; that thou be not seen of men to fast, but of thy Father which is in secret: and thy Father, which seeth in secret, shall recompense thee.

¶ Why beholdest thou the mote that is in thy brother's eye, but considerest not the beam that is in thine own eye? Or how canst thou say to thy brother, Brother, let me cast out the mote that is in thine eye, when thou thyself beholdest not the beam that is in thine own eye? Thou hypocrite, cast out first the beam out of thine own eye, and then shalt thou see clearly to cast out the mote that is in thy brother's eye.

¶ All things therefore whatsoever ye would that men should do unto you, even so do ye also unto them.

¶ Not every one that saith unto me, Lord, Lord, shall enter into the kingdom of God; but he that doeth the will of my Father.

¶ By their fruits ye shall know them. For of thorns men do not gather figs, nor of a bramble bush gather they grapes. Every good tree bringeth forth good fruit; but the corrupt tree bringeth forth evil fruit. A good tree cannot bring forth evil fruit, neither can a corrupt tree bring forth good fruit. The good man out of the good treasure of his heart bringeth forth that which is good; and the evil man out of the evil treasure bringeth forth that which is evil. Therefore by their fruits ye shall know them.

¶ Every one therefore which heareth these words of mine, and doeth them, shall be likened unto a wise man, which built his house upon the rock: and the rain descended, and the floods came, and the winds blew, and beat upon that house; and it fell not: for it was founded upon the rock. And every one that heareth these words of mine, and doeth them not, shall be likened unto a foolish man, which built his house upon the sand: and the rain descended, and the floods came, and the winds blew, and smote upon that house; and it fell: and great was the fall thereof.

Enter ye in by the narrow gate: for wide is the gate, and broad is the way, that leadeth to destruction, and many be they that enter in thereby. For narrow is the gate, and straitened the way, that leadeth unto life, and few be they that find it.

¶ And it came to pass, when Jesus ended these words, the multitudes were astonished at his teaching: for he taught them as one having authority, and not as their scribes.

Jesus' audience on this occasion is composed of what we would call the *disadvantaged class*—the poor people. They come to Jesus perhaps because he is one of them or at least on their side. They share a common enemy—the religious leaders. And if Jesus is indeed the Christ as rumour has it, then they want to be there *when it happens*!

Jesus says they are *blessed* (fortunate) presumably because they are open-minded and flexible and so able to hear and respond to his teaching.

The Pharisees left little doubt that they were the *Salt of the Earth*. The Scribes admitted that they were the *Light of the World*. Not so, says Jesus. It is those whose hearts and minds are open and receptive who merit that description.

The Pharisees who pride themselves on their

scrupulous observance of every detail of the Law and especially of the religious customs and practices, have charged Jesus with subversion—teaching the people disrespect for the Law and for accepted religious practices. Jesus denies the charge but instead of defending himself he attacks his accusers. He proceeds to show that their righteousness is mere mechanical rule-serving, superficial in its content and in large part motivated by the desire to impress people. He asserts that entrance into the Kingdom of God calls for a quality of righteousness away beyond anything his critics know about. To illustrate, he presents in turn examples of the Law which his critics take as their norm and then, going back to origins (as was his wont), shows that in each case the problem to be dealt with is not the overt act of killing, adultery, retaliation, etc., but the emotional state of the person [22, 19].

Thus, since it is anger that results in killing, the problem is anger. It is the anger that breaks one's relationship with God. Further, it is a break that remains as long as one is angry with anyone. Similarly in the matter of adultery, Jesus differentiates between the act and the thought that leads to the act.

It is the lustful thought, the desire to possess and use the other person that breaks the relationship with God. And Jesus feels strongly about this. Better to maim one's self if one cannot otherwise forego looking and touching with the accompanying fantasy, § 69.

Again, there is the matter of retaliation, *an eye*

for an eye—jungle justice, fighting back, defending one's self-image. For Jesus, the alternative to retaliation was non-retaliation, non-resistance. In our day, self-defence is approved but not retaliation. That would be *taking the law into one's own hands*. Instead, the state retaliates for us, thus maintaining *law and order* and social stability. But this does not automatically eliminate all thought of retaliation in the mind of the victim of the attack.

It was proper under Judaism to hate one's enemy. Jesus says No. Hate will drive out any awareness of God. To maintain that awareness one must love (care for) one's enemy; do good toward him as you do toward your friend. Treat everyone as God does—sun and rain on the good and on the bad—no discrimination. Be kind, be merciful, be helpful. Be like God.

The practice of oath-taking arose from the experience that, in general, people were not overly truthful. However, if one swore by God to tell the truth, then due to the sanction implied, one's veracity was thought to improve. Today we kiss the Jewish bible and swear that we will *tell the truth, the whole truth and nothing but the truth, so help me God!*

Jesus' alternative to oath-taking was simple—just tell the truth. No need to swear that you will be truthful if you are truthful already—committed to truth because truth is good, that is, *of God*.

Doing right acts (righteousness) publicly vs doing right acts privately—the one is seen by men but only God knows of the other. The motivation for the one is the enhancement of your public image as a religious person. The motivation for the other is the awareness of God's approval—the sense that you are doing what is right. So if you are committed to doing what is right, public approval is irrelevant—not a value.

The religious leaders have been criticizing Jesus. He suggests that it is better to defer criticism of others until you have carried self-criticism to the limit—a procedure which he himself had followed.

The religious leaders were morally blind because their minds were closed to any new insight. They rejected the *Counsel of God* when John confronted them and they came to Jesus' meetings not to listen and learn, but to find fault—to protect their system of values.

Having presented examples of what he saw as the right action for a number of problem situations, Jesus then offered a general guide for social behaviour. *All things therefore whatsoever ye would that men should do unto you even so do ye also unto them.*

According to this principle you have no need of an external ethical code to decide how to treat other people—you simply treat them as you would like yourself to be treated.

Would you like to be loved (cared for), accepted and treated as a fellow human being or be exploited, cheated, subjected to violence, discriminated against, treated as an object rather than a person? The norm is within your self. The principle is broad enough to cover all social situations.

Entrance into the Kingdom of God will not be achieved, Jesus said, by paying tribute to him. Nor does Jesus mention any special belief that you must hold about him as, for example, that he was the Christ. Certainly not that! But if one cannot enter the Kingdom of God by believing that Jesus was the Christ then how does one enter?!

The condition for entrance into the Kingdom of God may be stated simply—make God your King. This requires that henceforth, in every situation, at all times, you will do what you perceive is right —you will obey your conscience.

This is not the same thing as trying to live by the ethical standards enunciated by Jesus in this discourse. These were *his* insights. As he said, *the good man out of the good treasure of his heart bringeth forth that which is good.* Jesus could have these insights and he could act as he did because he was a *good man*, i.e., he was committed to doing what he perceived to be right, good. The value of these examples of ethical behaviour given in this discourse is that they may be seen as examples of the moral insights and behaviour of a *good man*. They were certainly never intended to be taken as a moral or ethical code for our guidance, applicable to all situations. Treated as such they are a constant source of frustration, self-recrimination and despair.

What we must realize and accept is that every human being is a unique individual in both nature and nurture. Our genes are unique and our accumulated life experience is unique. Because of our uniqueness, our insights—what our moral sense discriminates as to what it is good and proper for us to do in our particular situation—must also be unique. Every one of a hundred *good men* will make unique contributions to the growth and quality of the Kingdom of God. If I fail to become a *good man*, the contribution I could have made will never be made.

Jesus had the insights and did the things he did, not because he was merely unique—each of us is unique, but because he was a *good man*. How did he become a *good man*?

At the end of the discourse Jesus urged his listeners to respond—to act. He does not say *Everyone therefore which heareth these words of mine and believeth them*, but rather, *who heareth and doeth them*, shall be acting wisely. By *these words of mine* Jesus is obviously referring to the condition for entering the Kingdom of God. How did he, himself, make God his King?

Recall § 2. Jesus committed himself *in advance* to do God's will—the good, what is right. He was sincere about this, honest with himself, with no reservations. He thus became God's man.

This specification of the way to become a *good man* is experimentally verifiable. It is the *narrow gate* that *leadeth unto life*. Just one thing is required—to decide now that henceforth you will do whatever your moral sense tells you is good, right. That decision, consciously made, and resolutely followed is the one thing that is required.

The motivation for meeting this condition is paradoxically, quite selfish. It is that this route leads to fullness of life, wholeness for one's self.

CHAPTER 5

Contemporary Opinions About the Worth of Jesus

§18 Opinion of a Roman Centurion

AFTER Jesus had ended all his sayings in the ears of the people, he entered into Capernaum. And a certain centurion, when he heard concerning Jesus, sent unto him elders of the Jews, asking him that he would save his boy. And they, when they came to Jesus, besought him earnestly, saying, He is worthy that thou shouldest do this for him: for he loveth our nation, and himself built us our synagogue.

And Jesus went with them. And when he was now not far from the house, the centurion sent friends to him, saying unto him, Sir, trouble not thyself: for I am not worthy that thou shouldest come under my roof: wherefore neither thought I myself worthy to come unto thee: but say the word. For I also am a man set under authority, having under myself soldiers: and I say to this one, Go, and he goeth; and to another, Come, and he cometh; and to my servant, Do this, and he doeth it.

And when Jesus heard these things, he marvelled at the centurion, and turned and said unto the multitude that followed him, I say unto you, I have not found so great faith, no, not in Israel.

The centurion was a man of integrity who was sensitive and responsive to the values he found in subject peoples and their institutions. Since he was sympathetic to and accepted by the local Jewish Elders, he would have heard of their hopes and expectations concerning the coming of the Christ. And more recently he may have been told that the Christ has come and is travelling around the country teaching and performing cures.

Like Peter, § 7, *Depart from me, for I am a sinful man*, the centurion feels uneasy about going into the presence of one supposedly sent by God. However, he has no difficulty in believing that Jesus could effect a cure at a distance. His own commander has given him the authority to command and order action from those under him and he assumes that Jesus has authority from God to do likewise.

I have not seen so great faith, no, not in Israel. The great faith of the centurion which Jesus finds unique is not the man's acceptance of the possibility of action at a distance, a miracle, for at that time such credulity was normal. Rather it was his acceptance of Jesus as from God and his confidence that God would, through Jesus, help him.

§19 Opinion of John the Baptist

And the disciples of John told him of all these things. And John calling unto him two of his disciples sent them to Jesus, saying, Art thou he that cometh, or look we for another? And when the men were come unto Jesus, they said, John the Baptist hath sent us unto thee, saying, Art thou he that cometh, or look we for another?

And Jesus answered and said unto them, Go your way, and tell John what things ye have seen and heard. And blessed is he, whosoever shall find none occasion of stumbling in me.

And when the messengers of John were departed, Jesus began to say unto the multitudes concerning John, What went ye out into the wilderness to behold? a reed shaken with the wind? But what went ye out to see? a man clothed in soft raiment? Behold, they which are gorgeously apparelled, and live delicately, are in kings' courts. But what went ye out to see? a prophet? I say unto you, Among them that are born of women there is none greater than John: yet he that is but little in the kingdom of God is greater than John. He that hath ears to hear, let him hear.

From the days of John the Baptist until now the kingdom of God suffereth violence, and men of violence take it by force. For all the prophets and the law prophesied until John.

Whereunto then shall I liken the men of this generation, and to what are they like? They are like unto children that sit in the marketplace, and call one to another; which say, We piped unto you, and ye did not dance; we wailed, and ye did not weep. For John is come eating no bread nor drinking wine; and ye say, He hath a devil. I am come eating and drinking; and ye say, Behold, a gluttonous man, and a winebibber, a friend of publicans and sinners! And wisdom is justified of all her children.

Since up to this time there is no evidence that John had identified Jesus with the Christ, his question now was surely seeking confirmation of rumours to that effect which had come to him.

Jesus' answer: *Here is what I am doing, judge for your self,* carries also the warning, *do not be led astray by what you hear about me.* John was looking for a man from God, the Christ. Jesus was God's man by his own choice. Could John differentiate between these two on the basis of Jesus' activity?

In Jesus' opinion, John was a great man for he knew that righteousness was necessary to enter the Kingdom of God and he knew that the racial, political-Christ concept was wrong. But he believed in an apocalyptic Christ which involved the elimination of evil people by supernatural intervention as a prerequisite to the coming of the Kingdom of God. Jesus knew from personal experience that the coming of the Kingdom of God was dependent not on God's intervention but on man's decision to accept God (good) as his King. So John's shortcoming was that he didn't really understand what the Kingdom of God was or how it could come into being.

Up to the time of John, says Jesus, people supposed that obedience to the Law (conventional righteousness) was required for membership in the Kingdom of God. The requirement for admission to the Kingdom of God was known to Jesus, since his baptism by John, to be individual commitment to obey the Will of God—one's moral sense—to do what one conceived to be right.

Jesus goes on to describe *the men of this generation*, his critics. John came calling for repentance but the religious leaders *rejected for themselves the Counsel of God* and rationalized their position by affirming that John was crazy. And when Jesus came with a prophetic message, the religious leaders rejected him on the ground that he was a *bon vivant* and careless of the company he kept.

Jesus' perceptive remark: *Wisdom is justified of all her children* applies to ourselves no less. For we also believe that we are *children of wisdom*, acting wisely, and expect that the justifications (rationalizations) we give for our behaviour will be accepted at face value.

§20 Opinion of a Sinner *vs* Opinion of a Pharisee

And one of the Pharisees desired Jesus that he would eat with him. And Jesus entered into the Pharisee's house, and sat down to meat. And behold, a woman which was in the city, a sinner; and when she knew that Jesus was sitting at meat in the Pharisee's house, she brought an alabaster cruse of ointment, and standing behind at his feet, weeping, she began to wet his feet with her tears, and wiped them with the hair of her head, and kissed his feet, and anointed them with the ointment.
Now when the Pharisee which had bidden Jesus saw it, he spake within himself, saying, This man, if he were a prophet, would have perceived who and what manner of woman this is which toucheth him, that she is a sinner.
And Jesus answering said unto him, Simon, I have somewhat to say unto thee. And he saith, Teacher,

say on. Jesus said, A certain lender had two debtors: the one owed five hundred pence, and the other fifty. When they had not wherewith to pay, he forgave them both. Which of them therefore will love him most? Simon answered and said, He, I suppose, to whom he forgave the most. And Jesus said unto him, Thou hast rightly judged.
And turning to the woman, Jesus said unto Simon, Seest thou this woman? I entered into thine house; thou gavest me no water for my feet: but she hath wetted my feet with her tears, and wiped them with her hair. Thou gavest me no kiss: but she, since the time I came in, hath not ceased to kiss my feet. My head with oil thou didst not anoint: but she hath anointed my feet with ointment. Wherefore I say unto thee, Her sins, which are many, are forgiven; for she loved much.
And Jesus said unto the woman, Thy sins are forgiven. And they that sat at meat with him began to say within themselves, Who is this that even forgiveth sins? And he said unto the woman, Thy faith hath saved thee; go in peace.

Sometimes it is helpful to substitute the phrase *care for* for the word *love*; the phrase *confidence in God* for the word *faith* and the word *goodness* for the symbolic word *God* [25, 19].

The woman felt that Jesus was a good man and she showed by her actions that she cared about goodness (God). That attitude enabled Jesus to state that she was forgiven. She was saved by her awareness and confidence in goodness, God.

The Pharisee felt that Jesus could not possibly

be a prophet (man of God) because, by pharisaic standards, no religious person would permit a sinner (religious outcast) to touch him.

§21 Opinion of the Friends of Jesus

And Jesus cometh into a house. And the multitude cometh together again, so that they could not so much as eat bread. And when his friends heard it, they went out to lay hold on him: for they said, He is beside himself.

Beside himself—out of his wits or senses, crazy. The basis for such a conclusion was surely that Jesus, by his teaching, was increasingly antagonizing the religious leaders and this could only lead to trouble for him—an outcome which his friends believed any man in his right mind would carefully avoid.

§22 Opinion of the Religious Leaders

And Jesus was casting out a devil. And it came to pass that when the devil was gone out the multitudes marvelled. And the scribes which came down from Jerusalem said, He hath Beelzebub, and, By the prince of the devils casteth he out the devils.
And Jesus called them unto him, and said unto them, How can Satan cast out Satan? If a kingdom be divided against itself, that kingdom cannot stand but is brought to desolation. And every city or house divided against itself will not be able to stand, but falleth. And if Satan hath risen up against himself, and is divided, he cannot stand, but hath an end.

If I by Beelzebub cast out devils, by whom do your sons cast them out? Therefore shall they be your judges. Verily I say unto you, Whosoever shall speak a word against me, it shall be forgiven him; but whosoever shall blaspheme against the Spirit of God, it shall not be forgiven him. This was because they said, He hath an unclean spirit.

Jesus believed that he was wholly committed to God (the good) and believed that what he did was an expression of that commitment. The effort to help the unbalanced person was obviously a good act. For the Scribes to assert that the act springs from an evil source is to say that good is bad, right is wrong. This was a denial of their moral sense—*the Counsel of God*. If this attitude is persisted in, the ability to discriminate between good and evil must deteriorate and eventually be lost. In that case, repentance, which is a prerequisite to forgiveness and which requires that one turn again to the good (God), becomes impossible—the ship has lost its compass. Hence forgiveness is impossible for *blasphemy against the Spirit of God*.

It would appear from this report that exorcism was a common practice. The sons of the Pharisees also practised it.

CHAPTER 6

The Mystery of the Kingdom of God

§23 Basis of Real Relationship to Jesus

AND there come his mother and his brēthren; and, standing without, they sent unto Jesus, calling him. And a multitude was sitting about him; and they say unto him, Behold, thy mother and thy brēthren without seek for thee. And he answerēth them, and saith, Who is my mother and my brēthren? Whosoever shall do the will of God, the same is my brother, and siſter, and mother.

Since his mother and brothers were standing outside, Jesus as a member of a close-knit Jewish family was expected to go out and join them or bring them in. He did neither but raised a question about the fundamental basis of human relationships. What matters is not having the same blood but having the same purpose. When two people are individually committed to doing the Will of God—that is, committed to doing what each perceives to be right in his own situation, their relationship to one another must be the most basic. This simple situation was given this turn by Jesus because for him, the one relationship which was all important was his relationship to God. That was what filled his consciousness.

It is implied that everyone is a potential mother or brother to Jesus—that is, everyone has the human equipment required for learning what the Will of God is for him and the will to commit himself to do it.

§24 Discourse on the Kingdom of God

And again Jesus began to teach by the sea side. And there is gathered unto him a very great multitude, so that he entered into a boat, and sat in the sea; and all the multitude were by the sea on the land. And he taught them many things in parables, and said unto them in his teaching:

⁋ How shall we liken the kingdom of God? or in what parable shall we set it forth? It is like a grain of mustard seed, which, when it is sown upon the earth, though it be less than all the seeds that are upon the earth, yet when it is sown, groweth up, and becometh greater than all the herbs, and putteth out great branches; so that the birds of the heaven can lodge under the shadow thereof.

And again he said, Whereunto shall I liken the kingdom of God? It is like unto leaven, which a woman took and hid in three measures of meal, till it was all leavened.

And he said, Who hath ears to hear, let him hear.

⁋ Another parable set Jesus before them, saying, The kingdom of God is likened unto a man that sowed good seed in his field: but while men slept, his enemy came and sowed tares also among the wheat, and went

away. But when the blade sprang up, and brought forth fruit, then appeared the tares also. And the servants of the householder came and said unto him, Sir, didst thou not sow good seed in thy field? whence then hath it tares? And he said unto them, An enemy hath done this. And the servants say unto him, Wilt thou then that we go and gather them up? But he saith, Nay; lest haply while ye gather up the tares, ye root up the wheat with them. Let both grow together.
If any man hath ears to hear, let him hear.
⁋And Jesus said, So is the kingdom of God, as if a man should cast seed upon the earth; and should sleep and rise night and day, and the seed should spring up and grow, he knoweth not how. The earth beareth fruit of herself; first the blade, then the ear, then the full corn in the ear.
⁋The kingdom of God is like unto a treasure hidden in the field; which a man found, and hid; and in his joy he goeth and selleth all that he hath, and buyeth that field.
Again, the kingdom of God is like unto a man that is a merchant seeking goodly pearls: and having found one pearl of great price, he went and sold all that he had, and bought it.
He that hath ears, let him hear.
⁋And with many such parables spake Jesus the word unto them, as they were able to hear it: and without a parable spake he not unto them.
⁋And when Jesus was alone, the disciples came, and said unto him, Why speakest thou unto them in parables? And he said unto them, Unto you is given the mystery of the kingdom of God: but unto them that

are without, all things are done in parables: that seeing they may see, and not perceive; and hearing they may hear, and not understand.

Give not that which is holy unto the dogs, neither cast your pearls before the swine, lest haply they trample them under their feet, and turn and rend you.

¶ Then Jesus went into the house: and his disciples came unto him, saying, Explain unto us the parable of the tares of the field. And Jesus saith unto them, Know ye not this parable? and how shall ye know all the parables?

Take heed therefore how ye hear: for whosoever hath, to him shall be given; and whosoever hath not, from him shall be taken away even that which he thinketh he hath.

¶ Hearken: Behold, the sower went forth to sow: and it came to pass, as he sowed, some seed fell by the way side, and the birds came and devoured it. And other fell on the rocky ground, where it had not much earth; and straightway it sprang up, because it had no deepness of earth: and when the sun was risen, it was scorched; and because it had no root, it withered away. And other fell among the thorns, and the thorns grew up, and choked it, and it yielded no fruit. And others fell into the good ground, and yielded fruit, growing up and increasing; and brought forth, thirtyfold, and sixtyfold, and a hundredfold.

¶ And Jesus said unto them, Is the lamp brought to be put under the bushel, or under the bed, and not to be put on the stand? There is nothing hid, save that it should be manifested; neither was anything made secret, but that it should come to light.

¶And Jesus asked them, Have ye understood all these things? They say unto Jesus, Yea. And he said unto them, Therefore every scribe who hath been made a disciple to the kingdom of God is like unto a man that is a householder, which bringeth forth out of his treasure things new and old.

¶There is nothing covered up, that shall not be revealed: and hid, that shall not be known. What I tell you in the darkness, speak ye in the light: and what ye hear in the ear, proclaim upon the housetops. And I say unto you my friends, Be not afraid of them which kill the body, and after that have no more that they can do.

Among Jesus' discourses, this one, on the Kingdom of God, is distinctive. It is spoken entirely in parables. It is about a *mystery*. There is the repeated refrain, *Who hath ears to hear, let him hear*. But to Jesus' contemporaries the Kingdom of God was no mystery [20]. It was a concept which was fundamental though also controversial. All agreed that it would come when the Christ came. For some, as we have seen, the Kingdom of God would come through political action—the Christ would drive out the Romans and restore the reign of King David. It would be a kingdom for the sons of Abraham. For others, the coming of the Christ would signal the end of the Age, an age of righteousness would be inaugurated by a catastrophic event—a judgment, the separation of the good from the evil people and the destruction of the latter. That apocalyptic conception was held by John among others. Both conceptions would involve the miraculous intervention by God into the affairs of men. Both concepts held that the Kingdom of God was something objective in nature, observable, not subjective. It would be something seen and recognized. Events of significance might precede and lead to its establishment. Thus the recurrent question: *What will be the sign of its coming?*

From the language used in this discourse it seems clear that Jesus intended his own thought about the Kingdom of God to be less than obvious. The truth was being *put under a bushel; being hid; made secret.* Ultimately it was to be *put on the stand; made manifest; to come to light.*

So we may assume that what Jesus had to say on this theme was not what everybody knew, but something radically new and corrective of current conceptions. Such ideas are dangerous and Jesus protected himself by speaking in a form which would be a mystery to those whose minds were closed to new truths, but clear enough to those who were open-minded and discerning.

Thus we may test our understanding of the parables (stories with a central, focal point) by asking what current beliefs about the Kingdom of God were being corrected or negated by the parable.

1. *The Parable of the Mustard Seed:* The Kingdom of God has a very small beginning vs. the Kingdom of God will be large—full-blown at the outset.

2. *The Parable of the Leaven:* The Kingdom of

God comes about by a quiet, inner, transforming process, not readily observable vs. the coming of the Kingdom of God will be visible, observable by all.

3. *The Parable of the Tares:* The Kingdom of God can grow and develop in the presence of evil vs. the Kingdom of God will come following the destruction of all evil by the Christ. This was John's apocalyptic conception.

4. *The Parable of Growth:* The Kingdom of God grows naturally—a gradual, step-by-step unfolding vs. the Kingdom of God is imposed from without by supernatural intervention.

5. *The Parables of the Treasure and the Pearl:* These parables have in common the idea that the Kingdom of God is something of great value—all would agree with that. But the new truth found in these parables is that entrance into the Kingdom of God costs the individual *all that he has.* Thus Jesus' conception of entrance into the Kingdom of God was individual and, as we have seen earlier, involved total commitment *in advance* to do the Will of God [25]. Each individual man must choose to become subject to God. In the racial conception which is being corrected here, there was no admission charge for entrance into the Kingdom of God but only the children of Abraham were eligible.

6. *Parable of the Sower: The point here* is that the Kingdom of God is not for everybody but for the few—those who have the insight to understand the way and the determination to act with resolution.

Thus we see that Jesus' conception of the Kingdom of God was distinctive and quite different from that of his contemporaries. There were as he said, *things old and new*, but it was obviously the new ideas that justified the use of a teaching form that hid the intended truth from those whose minds were occupied with preconceptions and prejudice. To have spoken openly at that time would have been *counter-productive*, as we say, and indeed probably disastrous.

Jesus was concerned that his disciples should understand the *mystery*. He says: *unto you is given* and at the end he asks, *Have you understood?*

Jesus explained to his disciples that the truth was being concealed now but that later it would be for them to broadcast it in plain language. At the same time he warned them of the consequences of that procedure. *The dogs and swine* (religious leaders?) would not hesitate to destroy them. He himself was able to delay his destruction somewhat by the use of this parabolic form of teaching.

The Jews who held these Christly concepts were all involved with the same ultimate problem —the mode for the achievement of the rule of God among men. The Law, supposedly representing God's Will, was to be obeyed. God was to be King. The Jewish people, as his loyal subjects, would constitute his Kingdom. What was the obstacle to the realization of that supreme, national, religious ideal? Those who held the political concept said that the obstacle was the control of the state by Rome. Those who held the apocalyptic concept said that the obstacle was that there were evil people about—the Kingdom of God was to be composed of righteous people only. In each case the role of the Christ was to remove the obstacle which the Jews could not or would not remove by themselves.

Jesus may have thought that the religious problem should never have been considered as a national problem. A nation is an abstraction—it does not have a will. The individual has a will. If God is to rule, each person must decide to subject himself to God's rule. Thus God could still be King within an area where his rule is not imposed but accepted, even though that area is a kingdom less than a race or a nation. There could be a kingdom without large numbers. The parable of the Sower suggests that the subjects in the Kingdom will be few. *Few be they that find it.*

CHAPTER 7

Activity on Tours of Jesus and Disciples

§25 Fear *versus* Faith

Now it came to pass on one of those days, that Jesus entered into a boat, himself and his disciples; and he said unto them, Let us go over unto the other side of the lake. And leaving the multitude, they take him with them, even as he was, in the boat.
And there ariseth a great storm of wind, and the waves beat into the boat, insomuch that the boat was now filling. And he himself was in the stern, asleep on the cushion. And they awake him, and say unto him, Teacher, carest thou not that we perish?
And Jesus awoke, and said, Peace, be still. Why are ye fearful? have ye not yet faith?
And they came to the other side of the sea, into the country of the Gerasenes, which is over against Galilee.

The disciples, in a panic, assume that if Jesus were awake he could do something to prevent the boat from sinking. Jesus told them to be quiet and asked *Why are ye fearful, have ye not yet faith?* Clearly, one result of having faith [19] is a lack of fear, anxiety. Hence, being devoid of fear, you are able to see what the situation actually is and cope with it as, for example here, deal with a panic.

§26 Jesus Teaches at Nazareth

And when Jesus had crossed over again in the boat unto the other side, he cometh into his own country; and his disciples follow him. And when the sabbath was come, he began to teach in the synagogue.
And many hearing him were astonished, saying, Whence hath this man these things? and, What is the wisdom that is given unto this man? Is not this the carpenter, the son of Mary, and brother of James, and Joses, and Judas, and Simon? and are not his sisters here with us?
And they were offended in Jesus. And Jesus said unto them, A prophet is not without honour, save in his own country, and among his own kin, and in his own house.

The people of Nazareth who had known Jesus all his life and his parents and his brothers and sisters and had found nothing special about any of them—*all just like us*, were not prepared to believe that he had in a very short period of time become a different person with different interests and concerns and more especially with a striking, radical message. They ask *Whence hath this man these things!* § 2.
Presumably these simple village people took it for granted that wisdom lay with the priests and religious teachers. As we have seen, Jesus' fresh insights were the result of his having become God's man i.e. wholly committed to doing what he saw to be right in each situation.
Here for the first time we have Jesus' self-evaluation—he is a prophet. That no prophet finds

acceptance among his own people is surely due to closed minds and resentment. *Who does he think he is trying to tell me how to live?*

§27 Disciples Tour in Galilee

But when Jesus saw the multitudes, he saith unto his disciples, The harvest truly is plenteous, but the labourers are few. Pray ye therefore the Lord of the harvest, that he send forth labourers into his harvest.
And Jesus called unto him his twelve disciples, and began to send them forth by two and two. And he charged them that they should take nothing for their journey, save a staff only; no bread, no wallet, no money in their purse; for, said he, the labourer is worthy of his food.
And Jesus said unto them, Into whatsoever city or village ye shall enter, search out who in it is worthy. And as ye enter into the house, salute it. And if the house be worthy, let your peace come upon it. There abide till ye go forth, eating and drinking such things as they give. Go not from house to house.
He that receiveth you receiveth me, and he that receiveth me receiveth him that sent me.
And they went out, and preached that men should repent.

Since people were responding in such large numbers—whether to his message, his person or in the belief that he was the Christ, Jesus evidently felt that his message would get to more people if, instead of doing all the teaching himself, there were a group effort. So he decided to give his disciples responsibility. They were to set out without resources; to find in each village an open-minded, sympathetic family and stay there, eating what they were given. Going from house to house could result in too much hospitality and too little teaching.

He that receiveth you receiveth me and he that receiveth me, receiveth him that sent me. Jesus assumed the disciples would deliver the same message he would have delivered, a message he believed was from God.

§28 Fate of John the Baptist

At that season Herod the tetrarch heard the report concerning Jesus, and said unto his servants, This is John the Baptist, whom I beheaded; he is risen from the dead; and therefore do these powers work in him.
For Herod himself had sent forth and laid hold upon John, and bound him in prison. For John said unto Herod, It is not lawful for thee to have thy brother's wife. And for the sake of Herodias, his brother Philip's wife, Herod had sent and beheaded John in the prison.

John was a man of strong moral convictions with the courage to challenge even the most powerful in upholding his standards of conduct. Unfortunately, nothing was achieved by the brave act. This is an example of living by a code instead of by *every word that proceedeth out of the mouth of God.* John was a typical idealist seeking to impose an ideal solution on a problem situation. An individual with no official position or political power, John's stand cost him his life. Forty years later, when religious zealots, supported and encouraged by some of the religious leaders—people equally idealistic—sought to impose their ideal by challenging the rule of Rome, the Jewish state was destroyed [21].

The above examples of the consequences of idealism are not intended to show that there is something inherently wrong with a person who has ideals. Far from it. Being human beings we are able to *imagine* conditions, situations, behaviour which represent improvements over what now exists. Having ideals is thus an inescapable result of being human. However, *and this is the point*, it is always an error and self-defeating *to try to impose* one's ideals on other people. That is idealism.

§29 Report of Associates on Their Tour

And the twelve gather themselves together unto Jesus; and they told him all things, whatsoever they had done, and whatsoever they had taught. And he saith unto them, Come ye yourselves apart into a desert place, and rest a while. For there were many coming and going, and they had no leisure so much as to eat. And they went away in the boat to a desert place apart. And the people saw them going, and many knew them, and they ran there together on foot from all the cities, and outwent them.

And Jesus came forth and saw a great multitude, and he had compassion on them, because they were as sheep not having a shepherd: and he began to teach them many things.

And when the day was now far spent, Jesus constrained his disciples to enter into the boat, and to go before him unto the other side to Bēthsaida, while he himself sendēth the multitude away. And after he had taken leave of them, he departed into the mountain to pray.

The crowds were now even greater. It may well be that the disciples went about on their tour telling people that Jesus was the Christ and that they were his representatives. The fact that Jesus had to *constrain* his disciples to leave, suggests that having staged the show—that is, having invited people to come to see the Christ, they wanted to remain with the group for the prestige that would accrue to them. An entirely human situation.

As on previous occasions when he was faced with a new problem, Jesus withdrew to pray—that is, to seek insight on what to do next. Instead of being of assistance in spreading his message among the people, Jesus' disciples were becoming a liability.

CHAPTER 8

Demand by Pharisees for Conformity and Credentials

§30 Concerning Traditions about Defilement

AND there are gathered together unto Jesus the Pharisees, and certain of the scribes, which had come from Jerusalem, and had seen that some of his disciples ate their bread with defiled, that is, unwashen, hands.
For the Pharisees, and all the Jews, except they wash their hands diligently, eat not, holding the tradition of the elders: and when they come from the marketplace, except they wash themselves, they eat not: and many other things there be, which they have received to hold, washings of cups, and pots, and brasen vessels.
And the Pharisees and the scribes ask Jesus, Why walk not thy disciples according to the tradition of the elders, but eat their bread with defiled hands?
And Jesus said unto them, Well did Isaiah prophesy of you hypocrites, as it is written,
 This people honoureth me with their lips,
 But their heart is far from me.
 But in vain do they worship me,
 Teaching as their doctrines the precepts of men.

Ye leave the commandment of God, and hold fast the tradition of men.

And he said unto them, Full well do ye reject the commandment of God, that ye may keep your tradition. For Moses said, Honour thy father and thy mother; and, He that speaketh evil of father or mother, let him die the death: but ye say, If a man shall say to his father or his mother, That wherewith thou mightest have been profited by me is Corban, that is to say, Given to God; ye no longer suffer him to do aught for his father or his mother; making void the word of God by your tradition, which ye have delivered: and many such like things ye do.

¶ And Jesus called to him the multitude, and said unto them, Hear me all of you, and understand: To eat with unwashen hands defileth not the man. There is nothing from without the man, that going into him can defile him: but the things which proceed out of the man are those that defile the man.

¶ And when Jesus was entered into the house from the multitude, his disciples asked of him the parable. And he saith unto them, Are ye so without understanding also? Perceive ye not, that whatsoever from without goeth into the man, it cannot defile him; because it goeth not into his heart.

And he said, That which proceedeth out of the man, that defileth the man. For from within, out of the heart of men, evil thoughts proceed, fornications, thefts, murders, adulteries, covetings, wickednesses, deceit, lasciviousness, an evil eye, railing, pride, foolishness: all these evil things proceed from within, and defile the man.

DEMAND OF PHARISEES FOR CONFORMITY / 87

¶Then the disciples said unto Jesus, Knowest thou that the Pharisees were offended, when they heard that saying? But Jesus answered and said, Every plant which my Father planted not, shall be rooted up. Let them alone: they are blind guides. And if the blind guide the blind, both shall fall into a pit.

No doubt the washing of hands before eating had a sound basis in personal hygiene, but for the Pharisees, strict adherence to the purity regulations, inherited from the remote past, was not a matter of hygiene but of obedience, for the traditions of the Elders were regarded as also from God. Thus any departure from the custom of washing was thought to be offensive to God and hence *defiled* the man.

Jesus said that man *was not defiled* by eating with unwashed hands. This was a direct denial of the validity of the tradition. Jesus went on to say that it is man's evil thoughts that offend God and he illustrates by listing some of them. This was considered in § 17. Also see [22, 19].

On examining Jesus' list we see that the evil thoughts involve imagining—simulating murder, illicit sexual relations, retaliations, contemplating all manner of irresponsible, antisocial acts. Fortunately most of the acts so fantasized never take place though when they do the genesis of the murders, rapes, robberies, etc. is most likely in this earlier simulation. But that is not the point. *The point is* that indulging in such thoughts breaks one's relationship with God for in this condition, the conscience is submerged. In contrast, people who travel by the *narrow way* seek to be ever consciously aware of and responsive to the *Counsel of God* [25].

Every plant that my father planted not shall be rooted up. Jesus was quite confident that the *Counsel of God* would eventually replace the *traditions of men* as the norm for the individual's behaviour.

§31 Pharisees Demand Signs from Jesus

And the Pharisees came forth, and began to question with Jesus, seeking of him a sign from heaven. And he sighed deeply in his spirit, and saith, Why doth this generation seek a sign? An evil and adulterous generation seeketh after a sign. Verily I say unto you, There shall no sign be given unto this generation. And he left them, and again entering into the boat departed to the other side.

Many prophecies dealt with signs of the impending crisis—the coming of the Christ. There were to be signs among the nations, signs in Nature, significant conditions among the Jewish people, etc. The followers of Jesus were claiming that he was the Christ. The Pharisees no doubt assumed that Jesus believed himself to be that personage. So they, half in jest perhaps, ask for his credentials. If he is indeed the Christ, he can prove it to them by making a sign—performing a miracle perhaps.

This request surely raises a question about all the cases of miraculous healing Jesus was alleged to have been responsible for—not to mention walking on water, producing vast quantities of bread and fish on demand, etc. If all of these events or indeed any of them had actually occurred, what more sign was needed?

Having already castigated the Pharisees as hypocrites and blind guides, Jesus now places them in the context of *this evil and adulterous generation.* The sign that was there to be seen by those with *eyes to see and ears to hear* was Jesus himself with his radical new insight concerning the manner of the coming of the Kingdom of God. But the Scribes had said that Jesus was in league with Beelzebub. People thus perverted will see nothing. There will be no sign.

§32 The Leaven of the Pharisees

And Jesus charged his disciples, saying, Take heed, beware of the leaven of the Pharisees and the leaven of Herod. And they reasoned one with another, saying, We have no bread.
Jesus perceiving it saith unto them, Why reason ye, because ye have no bread? do ye not yet perceive, neither understand? have ye your heart hardened? Having eyes, see ye not? and having ears, hear ye not?
And he said unto them, Do ye not yet understand? How is it that ye do not perceive that I spake not to you concerning bread? But beware of the leaven of the Pharisees and Sadducees. Then understood they how

that he bade them not beware of the leaven of bread, but of the teaching of the Pharisees and Sadducees.

The leaven of Herod, of the Herodians and of the Sadducees was that the Kingdom of God was to be equated with the status quo. The leaven of the Pharisees was that the Kingdom of God would come when everyone kept the Law—i. e. was righteous—like the Pharisees.

CHAPTER 9

Forecast of Conflict with the Jerusalem Authorities

§33 Opinion of Disciples about Jesus

AND Jesus went forth, and his disciples, into the villages of Cæsarea Philippi: and in the way he asked his disciples, saying unto them, Who do men say that I am? And they told him, saying, John the Baptist: and others, Elijah; but others, One of the prophets. And Jesus asked them, But who say ye that I am? Peter answereth and saith unto him, Thou art the Christ. Then charged Jesus the disciples that they should tell no man that he was the Christ.

The identification of Jesus with the Christ concept appears from the record to have been very widespread and was responsible in large measure for the crowds of people who came to see and hear him wherever he went.

We have seen Jesus' position relative to this concept in § 3 and also his efforts to correct this error of identification. Here he raises the question directly with his disciples. *Who say men that I am?* And then, more importantly, *But who say ye that I am?* He knew the answer to that question but it was necessary to have it first-hand from the disciples themselves.

Peter's unhesitating reply not only makes it clear that Jesus' own close followers were convinced that he was the Christ but strongly suggests that they may have been largely responsible for the spreading of the idea in the first place.

Jesus ordered them to stop telling people that he was the Christ but clearly that was not enough— he had said that before. Now he must go further.

§34 Jesus Forecasts Events at Jerusalem

From that time began Jesus to shew unto his disciples, how that he must go unto Jerusalem, and be rejected by the elders and chief priests and scribes, and be delivered up into the hands of men, and be condemned to death, and suffer many things, and be set at nought, and be killed.
And Peter took him, and began to rebuke him, saying, Be it far from thee, Master: this shall never be unto thee. But Jesus turned, and said unto Peter, Get thee behind me, Satan: thou mindest not the things of God, but the things of men.

The fate which Jesus saw awaiting him in Jerusalem was to be expected from the growing opposition of the religious authorities. This antagonism was due to the fact that Jesus' teaching undermined their most basic religious position.

Jesus' picture of events in Jerusalem as something tragic and deplorable was very hard for his disciples and especially for Peter to accept, imagining as they had, his arrival in the capital city in triumph as the Christ—and they, his closest followers, in the centre of that stupendous event!

Thou mindest the things of men (prestige, status, power), *Thou mindest not the things of God* (goodness, truthfulness, doing right). *Get thee behind me Satan!* In view of Jesus' estimate of Peter, Peter's estimate of Jesus—*Thou art the Christ,* cannot be taken very seriously, § 3.

Obviously Jesus is here making a strong effort to get the disciples to see clearly that he is not as they thought the Christ—a notion that had preoccupied their minds from the beginning and prevented them from understanding his teaching and hence from being helpful in his mission.

§35 Some Costs of Discipleship

And Jesus called unto him the multitude with his disciples, and said unto them,
If any man would come after me, let him deny himself.
Whosoever would save his life shall lose it; but whosoever shall lose his life shall save it.
What is a man profited, if he gain the whole world, and lose or forfeit his own self?

Instead of becoming assistants who were *in the know* and so able to answer questions and even *spread the word*, the disciples had become a liability, making Jesus' efforts to counteract the ill-effect of the *leaven of the Pharisees* all the more difficult. So Jesus states in a new form, the condition for discipleship—*Let him deny himself.* This does not say deny something to the self but to deny the self outright as a self.

To deny to one's self a specific thing is to decide

not to have that thing, but to deny the self, as such, is to give up the freedom to decide what one will do. This is a radical demand. For the self (psyche) is the centre of the person; that which strives to continue to be—to survive in a hazardous, precarious environment. It has been the *zest for life* of this striving, struggling entity, the Self, that has brought the human race to this state of development, at this point in history—after millions of years evolving from some lesser form. To deny the self then would seem to be to capitulate, to give up the struggle, to sink into the abyss. And so it is! But done rightly something comes of it.

Whosoever would save his life shall lose it; but Whosoever shall lose his life shall save it.

A. E. Housman, Poet, Classical scholar and Fellow of Trinity College, Cambridge, said of Jesus' Paradox, *This is the most important truth ever uttered and the greatest discovery ever made.*

Jesus' paradoxical statement does not negate the ambition to possess fullness of life. What it does is to define the wrong process and the right process for achieving that end.

First Part: *Whosoever would save his life shall lose it.*
The process here is: *Would save his life.*
The outcome here is: *Shall lose his life.*
Second Part: *Whosoever shall lose his life, shall save it.*

The process here is: Shall lose his life.
The outcome here is: *Shall save his life.*

Thus the process in the first part is the outcome in the second part and the process in the second part is the outcome in the first part. The outcome in the second part is *life*—self-fulfillment. The motive for *losing one's life* is *to save one's life.* The motive is obviously selfish. This is not condemned. However, one may be frustrated in the effort to achieve the desired end by using the wrong process, by confusing ends and means.

Since what is desired is the outcome in the second part, the important thing is to determine the meaning of the phrase, *lose one's life* i.e. the process in the second part.

Some of the things this process does *not* mean are: (a) to lose the physical life for a person or a cause; (b) to lose oneself in service to others; (c) to become utterly possessed by the pursuit of some calling or some ambition or aim; (d) to enter into some profound mystical experience. It does not mean any of these things and that narrows the field a good deal.

To start with, suppose we examine the process in the first part of the saying—the wrong method. What does *save his life* as process mean? Perhaps we can understand what is meant by the wrong process if we look at ourselves and the people around us generally and ask: What are we doing and why? What is the outcome sooner or later of what we are doing? Is it fullness of life or frustration and emptiness?

We all crave material security because we believe that would result in our *feeling* secure. We accept the conventional prescriptions for success in that quest. But unless we are clever and unscrupulous or affiliated with groups which have able leaders and political power, we fall behind in the race and become submerged in the system.

What to do now? Rationalize our failure; blame our Union leaders or THAT MAN in the Government. Pretend it didn't happen. Escape into fantasy where the loser can still be a winner. Seek distractions of one sort or another. Drugs as varied as caffein, nicotine and cocaine are available to ease the sense of failure. The billion dollar business of sexploitation eagerly solicits our indulgence. The porno-industry encourages us to explore our erogenous zones, which we do. Orgasm *qua* orgasm. Is this self realization, or merely a sordid perversion of a normal bodily function? An escape from tension perhaps—but does it ease our anxiety or empty the well of loneliness?

And the achievers—whether by stealth or superior performance—are they so much better off? *What is a man profited if he gain the whole world and lose his own soul?* Be successful in the ratrace but become a rat. *Gain the whole world*—wrong process. *Lose his own soul*—undesired outcome.

None of the prescriptions really works for the disease has been wrongly diagnosed. The sense of security we seek calls for an inner adjustment [25].

Recall Jesus' experience at his baptism. His repentance and decision to change his life resulted in his having a sense that he had become God's man. *This day have I begotten thee*, § 2. From that point on he had a sense of security. It resulted from his complete surrender of the direction of his life to God's direction—a commitment *in advance* always to do what his moral sense told him was good, right, in each situation. *That is the meaning of the process, lose his life.*

Dr. Sharman once made the following statement about Jesus' Paradox: "In the teaching of Jesus there is disclosed a principle, a Law, which accounts for His life—a Law transcendently brought to expression in that immortal utterance —If any man seeks to maintain his autonomy unimpaired, he will destroy himself, but if any man will capitulate, will utterly abdicate, he shall attain to the conquering utilization of his essential self . . . The total personality confronted by and totally respondent to the totality of goodness which is God." (37).

The person who decides to *lose his life*—to turn over complete control of it to God—that is, decides to do henceforth whatever his moral sense tells him is right, does so because in that way and only in that way can he become a unified, whole person—a secure person, a person who knows who he is and what he is doing and who wants to be doing what he is doing and so does it freely and joyously. That is why one seeks to *lose one's life*. It is in order that one may live more fully, more abundantly. This is a way that is experimentally verifiable. Try it. You have nothing to lose but your anxiety and fear and dependence on all manner of questionable, external props. Take a permanent vacation from all that. *Live it up* with your moral sense. You will never find a more dependable companion!

Tertiaronomy

Jesus' Paradox is the Tertiaronomy—the third giving of the Law. But this giving is a Law of human nature which Jesus discovered and enunciated. The Paradox sets forth in two parts the conditions for human disintegration and integration. Unlike Deuteronomy which was allegedly of Divine origin and sanction, Tertiaronomy is of natural origin and sanction. Under Tertiaronomy, the individual is free to choose—to meet the condition for integration or to just ignore the challenge. To ignore the challenge encourages the illusion that one can remain as one is, but that is impossible. To face the challenge and to strive to meet the condition for integration is to experience a sense of wholeness and a new awareness of what it means to be fully alive. To evade the challenge is to incur the resulting progressive deterioration of selfhood.

§36 The Problem of Tribute Payment

And when they were come to Capernaum, they that received the half-shekel came to Pêter, and said, Doth not your teacher pay the half-shekel? He saith, Yea. And when he came into the house, Jesus spake first to

him, saying, What thinkest thou, Simon? the kings of the earth, from whom do they receive toll or tribute? from their sons, or from strangers? And when he said, From strangers, Jesus said unto him, Therefore the sons are free.
But, lest we cause them to stumble, go thou to the sea, and cast a hook, and take up the fish that first cometh up: that take, and give unto them for me and thee.

The *half-shekel* was an annual poll-tax for the maintenance of the public cultus in the temple in Jerusalem. All Jews were supposed to pay it. It was the conventional right thing to do and so Peter commits Jesus to paying the tax.

Jesus argues by analogy with the kingdoms of the earth that the sons of that other kingdom are also free—to pay or not to pay—whatever is right. And here it is right to pay, for the tax collector would not understand about that other kingdom whose sons are free because they are all volunteers. So, says Jesus, we will pay the tax. In fact Peter, since you committed us to payment—you pay it!

§37 Teaching on Greatness

And when Jesus was in the house at Capernaum, he asked them, What were ye reasoning in the way? But they held their peace: for they had disputed one with another in the way, who was the greatest.
And Jesus sat down, and called the twelve; and he saith unto them, If any man would be first, he shall be last of all, and minister of all.

Salt is good: but if the salt have lost its saltness, wherewith will ye season it? Have salt in yourselves, and be at peace one with another.

Salt is good . . . have salt in yourselves. In the discourse on righteousness, § 17, Jesus said that the disciples were the *Salt of the Earth.* Here he has reason to believe that his earlier estimate of the quality of the disciples may have been mistaken.

If any man would be first, he shall be last of all and minister of all. Jesus does not condemn the desire for place and power but rather suggests a sound method for achieving it. However, it must be pointed out that the method for becoming great among men has nothing in common with the method for achieving fullness of life.

§38 Teaching on Tolerance

John said unto Jesus, Teacher, we saw one casting out devils in thy name: and we forbade him, because he followed not with us. But Jesus said, Forbid him not: for there is no man which shall do a mighty work in my name, and be able quickly to speak evil of me. For he that is not against us is for us.

Evidently exorcism was a fairly common practice at the time. However, due to the fact that Jesus was alleged to be the Christ, the use of his name in the practice of *casting out devils* would seem likely to increase the success of the practitioners.

We forbade him because he followed not us. A typical example of the intolerance found all down the ages among members of competing religious sects.

Jesus' comment: If the use of my name contributed to the man's success, he will feel friendly toward us. Do not discourage him. We need all the friends we can get.

§39 Teaching on Forgiveness

And Jesus said unto his disciples, Take heed to yourselves: if thy brother sin, rebuke him; and if he repent, forgive him. And if he sin against thee seven times in the day, and seven times turn again to thee, saying, I repent; thou shalt forgive him.
Then came Peter, and said to Jesus, How oft shall my brother sin against me, Master, and I forgive him? until seven times? Jesus saith unto him, I say not unto thee, Until seven times; but, Until seventy times seven.

Obviously it is the forgiving person who is benefitted by the repeated *until seventy times seven* forgiveness. For, as we found in § 17, failure to forgive another person who has wronged you prevents you from being able to maintain your own relationship with God [19]. Forgiving the offender, regardless of whether or not he is repentant, is therefore essential. It may have no effect at all on the offender. The restoration of his relationship with God is his problem.

§40 Parable on Forgiveness

A certain king would make a reckoning with his servants. And when he had begun to reckon, one was brought unto him, which owed him ten thousand

talents. But forasmuch as he had not wherewith to pay, his master commanded him to be sold, and his wife, and children, and all that he had, and payment to be made. The servant therefore fell down and worshipped him, saying, Master, have patience with me, and I will pay thee all. And the master of that servant, being moved with compassion, released him, and forgave him the debt.
But that servant went out, and found one of his fellow-servants, which owed him a hundred pence: and he laid hold on him, and took him by the throat, saying, Pay what thou owest. So his fellow-servant fell down and besought him, saying, Have patience with me, and I will pay thee. And he would not: but went and cast him into prison, till he should pay that which was due.
So when his fellow-servants saw what was done, they were exceeding sorry, and came and told unto their master all that was done. Then his master called him unto him, and saith to him, Thou wicked servant, I forgave thee all that debt, because thou besoughtest me: shouldest not thou also have had mercy on thy fellow-servant, even as I had mercy on thee?

The point here is that if a person who is in debt to God, that is, is a sinner, asks God to forgive him, he will be forgiven. The proper attitude for a person who has been wronged, toward the person who has wronged him, is one of mercy. The basis for this statement is that this is God's attitude toward the wrong-doer.

CHAPTER 10

Departure from Galilee for Jerusalem

§41 General Statement of Journey

AND it came to pass when Jesus had finished these words, he departed from Galilee. And multitudes come together unto him again; and, as he was wont, he taught them.
And when the days were well-nigh come that he should be received up, Jesus stedfastly set his face to go to Jerusalem.

Apart from the two discourses so far reported, we have no information concerning the theme of Jesus' teaching in the many places where he is reported to have taught. However, when one recalls that there were no tape-recorders, nor short-hand recording, nor typists, but only memory to retain the spoken word and, after many years, that but dimly, the surprising thing is that we have so much.
Having in mind Jesus' forecast to Peter of probable events when he reached Jerusalem, the statement that he *steadfastly set his face* is understandable. The future looked grim.

§42 Teaching on Tolerance

And Jesus sent messengers before his face: and they went, and entered into a village of the Samaritans, to make ready for him. And they did not receive him, because his face was as though he were going to Jerusalem. And when his disciples James and John saw this, they said, Master, wilt thou that we bid fire to come down from heaven, and consume them? But Jesus turned, and rebuked them, and said, Ye know not what manner of spirit ye are of. And they went to another village.

As though he were going to Jerusalem. Jews and Samaritans were enemies and since anyone going to Jerusalem was likely to be a Jew, the attitude of the Samaritans was probably as reported.

Wilt thou that we bid fire to come down from heaven and consume them? The toleration of people for others whose beliefs differ markedly from their own has never been a striking feature of the attitude of competing religious groups. While the Christian Church has not been alone in its intolerance, it has been outstanding. Tuchman (7) traces the roots of anti-semitism to the attitude of the early church toward the Jews who refused to accept the crucified Jesus as the Christ.

As against the ostracism or persecution or overt acts toward those who oppose, the constructive method of dealing with opposition as illustrated by this incident would appear to be to *go to another village* i.e. *resist not evil*, avoid it. The important state of homeostasis is thus maintained [19].

But Jesus did not follow a rigid rule—what is the right thing to do in one situation is not necessarily the right thing to do in another. In his encounters with his critics the Scribes and Pharisees, Jesus avoided confrontation as much as possible but as it became clear that their minds were closed and that their beliefs concerning the future were dangerously misleading, he was no longer tolerant. On the contrary, he denounced them as blind guides and hypocrites and warned the people of the disastrous consequences of following them.

The notion of the disciples that, with Jesus' approval, fire could be called down from heaven, indicates how completely convinced they were that Jesus was the Christ, God's agent, and hence had access to supernatural power. Jesus rebuked them for their intolerance. His concluding remark —*Ye know not what manner of spirit ye are of* is reminiscent of that exchange between Glendower and Hotspur in Shakespear's Henry the Fourth, (8):

Glendower—I can call spirits from the vasty deep.

Hotspur— Why so can I, or so can any man, but will they come when you do call them?

§43 Some Tests of Discipleship

And as they went in the way, a certain man said unto Jesus, I will follow thee whithersoever thou goest. And Jesus said unto him, The foxes have holes, and the birds of the heaven have lodging-places; but I have not where to lay my head.

And Jesus said unto another, Follow me. But he said, Suffer me first to go and bury my father. But Jesus said unto him, Leave the dead to bury their own dead. And another also said, I will follow thee, Master; but first suffer me to bid farewell to them that are at my house. But Jesus said unto him, No man, having put his hand to the plough, and looking back, is fit for the kingdom of God.

Have not where to lay my head. Becoming a follower of Jesus, it should be understood, does not guarantee that one's physical needs will be taken care of. At this late stage in his public career Jesus evidently wanted prospective followers to understand that the personal cost of association with his movement was very high.

Leave the dead to bury their own dead. Let the *wide-gaters* bury the *wide-gaters* when they die. The *narrow-gaters* have more important work to do, § 17.

No man, having set his hand to the plow and looking back is fit for the Kingdom of God. If a man has committed himself to doing the Will of God (the good), but later changes his mind, he clearly still lacks the essential quality for that undertaking.

§44 The Way of Eternal Life

And behold, a certain lawyer stood up and questioned Jesus, saying, Teacher, what shall I do to inherit eternal life? And Jesus said unto him, What is written in the law? how readest thou? And he answering said, Thou shalt love the Lord thy God with all thy heart, and with all thy soul, and with all thy strength, and with all thy mind; and thy neighbour as thyself. And Jesus said unto him, Thou hast answered right: this do, and thou shalt live.

The lawyer quoted two laws from two widely separated books of the Jewish scripture (Deuteronomy 6:5 and Leviticus 19:18). To have brought them together indicates a considerable amount of insight. One law has to do with one's relationship with God: the other with one's relationship with one's fellow men.

All thy heart (emotions) *and all thy soul* (psyche) *and all thy strength* (body) *and all thy mind* (reason, intuitive faculty). All, all, all and all which adds up to the whole person. See also § 80. If we read *love* to mean *care for*, the law says *Thou shalt care for God* (goodness, truth, rightness) *with the whole personality.*

The second law—*Thou shalt love thy neighbor as thy self* is an ethical rule for deciding how to treat your neighbor. According to this rule, the norm or standard is within yourself—no external code is required.

This do and thou shalt live. The lawyer had derived his definition of the way to life from his own books of religion and Jesus had accepted that definition as completely adequate. The only contribution Jesus made was to indicate that the goal *life* would not be had by mere understanding of the way. The lawyer must *do*, i.e. must base his day-to-day living upon these laws.

Thou shalt love thy neighbor as thyself. In § 17

there was a saying by Jesus having the same meaning—*All things therefore whatsoever ye would that men should do unto you even so do ye also unto them.*

According to the scripture quoted by the lawyer, *Love thy neighbor as thyself,* there is nothing wrong with loving one's self. Perhaps our trouble is that we do not care enough for our selves. If a person cares supremely about himself he will surely be willing to do whatever is required in order to live fully—to get the most possible out of life.

Jesus' Way to Life does not call for unselfishness but for selflessness. One must have a great zest for life—want the very best there is for one's self—be willing to become selfless as a means to one's selfish end. Apparently that zest, that yearning for and willingness to pay the cost of the best which life afforded was rare in Jesus' day for, as he observed, *few be they that find it.* Is it otherwise in our own day?

Christians have been led astray by those who have held that unselfishness was not only a virtue but the virtue most to be cultivated. But lacking any knowledge or understanding of Jesus' *Way to Life*, perhaps the confusion between unselfishness and selflessness, as process, is understandable.

He who *seeks to lose his life* though he do it for the most selfish reasons will, because his own basic need is satisfied, find himself interested in other people; able to understand and help them and care for their welfare no less than for his own.

For the *good man*, loving his neighbor as himself is whole-hearted and spontaneous. For others, it is impossible.

§45 The Definition of Neighbour

A certain lawyer said unto Jesus, Who is my neighbour? Jesus made answer and said, A certain man was going down from Jerusalem to Jericho; and he fell among robbers, which both stripped him and beat him, and departed, leaving him half dead. And by chance a certain priest was going down that way: and when he saw him, he passed by on the other side. And in like manner a Levite also, when he came to the place, and saw him, passed by on the other side. But a certain Samaritan, as he journeyed, came where he was: and when he saw him, he was moved with compassion, and came to him, and bound up his wounds, pouring on them oil and wine; and he set him on his own beast, and brought him to an inn, and took care of him. And on the morrow he took out some money, and gave it to the host, and said, Take care of him; and whatsoever thou spendest more, I, when I come back again, will repay thee.
Which of these three, thinkest thou, proved neighbour unto him that fell among the robbers? And he said, He that shewed mercy on him. And Jesus said unto him, Go, and do thou likewise.

According to Jesus, the neighbor is anyone who is in need. However the Jewish scripture (Leviticus 19:17-18) defined neighbor as a fellow Jew. To have answered the enquiring lawyer by saying that the definition of neighbor found in the scriptures was wrong would have been unhelpful to say the least. Instead, Jesus achieved the same result by telling a story and having the lawyer decide for himself who acted in a neighborly manner.

By using the Samaritan, a non-Jew and regarded as an enemy by the Jews, as the character who acts neighborly, Jesus enlarges the concept of neighbor to mean one who acts in a certain way—shows compassion in case of need. The scriptural definition—the neighbor of a Jew is a Jew—is thus shown to be too limiting.

§46 Many Things *vs* One Thing

Now as they went on their way, Jesus entered into a certain village: and a certain woman named Martha received him into her house. And she had a sister called Mary, which also sat at the Master's feet, and heard his word. But Martha was cumbered about much serving; and she came up to him, and said, Master, dost thou not care that my sister did leave me to serve alone? bid her therefore that she help me. But the Master answered and said unto her, Martha, Martha, thou art anxious and troubled about many things: but one thing is needful.

The one thing that is needful, according to Jesus, is to lose or deny the self. This incident was trivial and commonplace but Jesus turned it into something profound, reflecting his constant awareness of his own commitment.

§47 Elements of Prevailing Prayer

And it came to pass, as Jesus was praying in a certain place, that when he ceased, one of his disciples said unto him, Master, teach us to pray, even as John also taught his disciples.

And Jesus said unto them, In praying use not vain repetitions, as the Gentiles do: for they think that they shall be heard for their much speaking. Be not therefore like unto them: for God your Father knoweth what things ye have need of, before ye ask him.

After this manner therefore pray ye:
Father,
Hallowed be thy name.
Thy kingdom come.
Thy will be done, as in heaven, so on earth.
Give us day by day our daily bread.
And forgive us our sins; for we ourselves also forgive every one who has wronged us.

Therefore I say unto you, Whensoever ye stand praying, forgive, if ye have aught against any one; that your Father also may forgive you your trespasses.

And I say unto you, Ask, and it shall be given you; seek, and ye shall find; knock, and it shall be opened unto you. For every one that asketh receiveth; and he that seeketh findeth; and to him that knocketh it shall be opened.

And of which of you that is a father shall his son ask a loaf, and he give him a stone? or a fish, and he for a fish give him a serpent? Or if he shall ask an egg, will he give him a scorpion? If ye then, being evil, know how to give good gifts unto your children, how much

more shall your Father give good things to them that ask him?
All things whatsoever ye pray and ask for, believe that ye have received them, and ye shall have them.

God knoweth what things ye have need of before ye ask him. Hence God needs neither to be informed nor persuaded. The validity and value of prayer is that by that means the one who prays achieves a suitable psychological state for learning something—a state of awareness and receptivity. Insight comes from within when this condition is met, § 87 [25].

But for God to forgive the sins of the petitioner, he, the petitioner, must already have forgiven anyone who had in any way wronged him. This is a requirement or law of forgiveness because it is necessary psychologically if the person is to be detached and open to fresh insight. How can you learn what is good (of God) if you still hate some one—have a closed mind? [19]

The central and most significant petition within the prayer is surely *Thy will be done, as in heaven, so on earth.* This is the process for which the outcome is *Thy Kingdom Come.*

One reads of people passively accepting as *God's Will* all manner of random events in which they happen to have been involved, purely by chance. The *Will of God* is rather the directive for action given by our moral sense. It has to do with events which have yet to happen [25].

The person who through prayer is trying to find out what the Will of God is for himself in a particular situation, will *ask, seek, knock*—that is, will persist in his search until he finds an answer. His fundamental attitude must be one of willingness to do the Will of God (the good, what is right) when he finds it, regardless of what it may be.

The antithesis of this attitude is that of asking God for special favours—specific changes in a situation. This is actually a request for an intervention into the Natural order. It is futile. There are none. God is a non-intervenor, [24] § 3.

How much more shall your Father give good things? Those who persist in the search for insight concerning what is the right thing to do will receive an answer. This is a plea for trust in God (in one's own moral sense).

Believe that ye have received them and ye shall have them. Insight comes from within as we know. Better believe that it is there and that it will come. But it cannot come out of a vacuum. If you are to gain insight on a problem (what is the right thing to do now?) the brain must be saturated with knowledge—all that you can learn about the problem. Having given the brain something to work on, you must wait, confident that insight will come. But the precondition for insight is that you be committed in advance to respect what comes; to take it seriously and to act upon it when you are sure it is right. For insight thus obtained is not exempt from examination by your critical faculty. It must be checked. If you are not sure that you now know what is the right thing to do, you must re-examine your commitment and seek further. We have to be honest with ourselves.

§48 Limitations of Exorcism

And Jesus was casting out a devil. And it came to pass, when the devil was gone out, Jesus said,
The unclean spirit, when he is gone out of the man, passeth through waterless places, seeking rest, and findeth it not. Then he saith, I will return into my house whence I came out; and when he is come, he findeth it empty, swept, and garnished. Then goeth he, and taketh with himself seven other spirits more evil than himself, and they enter in and dwell there: and the last state of that man becometh worse than the first.

It would seem that what help Jesus was able to give to disturbed people was short-term and that he had no illusions that he was effecting a permanent cure. On the contrary, he evidently believed that the person would probably get worse, which explains, perhaps, why he avoided that activity as much as possible.

§49 Basis of Real Relationship to Jesus

And it came to pass, as Jesus said these things, a certain woman out of the multitude lifted up her voice, and said unto him, Blessed is the womb that bare thee, and the breasts which thou didst suck. But Jesus said, Yea rather, blessed are they that hear the word of God, and keep it.

To hear *the word of God* is to be aware of the intimations of one's moral sense—what else? *And keep it*—do it—obey the *Counsel of God*, one's conscience. This was primary with Jesus [25].

Jesus' attitude here does not support the notion that having Mary as his mother had any special significance.

CHAPTER 11

Deep Feeling and Direct Teaching

§50 Effects of the Mission of Jesus

IN THE mean time, when the many thousands of the multitude were gathered together, insomuch that they trode one upon another, Jesus began to say unto his disciples first of all,
Think ye that I am come to cast peace on the earth? I tell you, Nay; but rather division: for there shall be from henceforth five in one house divided, three against two, and two against three. They shall be divided, father against son, and son against father; mother against daughter, and daughter against her mother; mother in law against her daughter in law, and daughter in law against her mother in law. And a man's foes shall be they of his own household.
I came to cast fire upon the earth; and what will I, if it is already kindled? But I have a baptism to be baptized with; and how am I straitened till it be accomplished!

Think ye that I came to cast peace on the earth? I tell you nay, but rather division. In the light of this statement there seems little justification for regarding Jesus as a *Prince of Peace.*
A man's foes shall be those of his own household. There will be division between those who

adhere to the old outlook and the values of the religious leaders and those who, *having eyes to see and ears to hear*, have understood, accepted and tested the new teaching.

I came to cast fire upon the earth. The new teaching has shown that the contemporary conceptions of how the Kingdom of God is to come are wrong. It has eliminated the need for *whole burnt offerings and sacrifices* as prerequisites to forgiveness. *Man hath power on earth to forgive sins.* It has cast doubt on many of the current religious practices and customs. It has shown that the Kingdom of God grows by individual increments rather than being imposed and that any individual who is prepared to pay the price, *lose his life*, may enter.

I have a baptism to be baptised with. Jesus is here referring to his rejection (by the religious leaders) and his probable death in Jerusalem at the hands of those same religious leaders. The inevitability of this is becoming painfully apparent to him. In spite of that, his attitude toward the future is that he will continue doing what for him is the right thing. He will go on with his teaching as long as he is free to do so.

§51 The Signs of the Times

And Jesus said to the multitudes also, When ye see a cloud rising in the west, straightway ye say, There cometh a shower; and so it cometh to pass. And when ye see a south wind blowing, ye say, There will be a scorching heat; and it cometh to pass. Ye know how to interpret the face of the earth and the heaven; but how is it that ye cannot discern the signs of the times?

How is it that ye cannot discern the signs of the times! The religious leaders, Scribes and Pharisees, could not see what was going on around them for they, or most of them, were preoccupied with their conventional activities. Some, a minority perhaps, were actively supporting the Zealots who, believing that the Christ would come and drive out the Romans and then usher in God's Kingdom, undertook to initiate the anti-Rome campaign themselves. Their active effort to impose that ideal solution upon the historical situation was being met with savage reprisals by the Roman authorities [21].

These were the signs of the times which Jesus saw. He had decided at the beginning of his career that political Messianism was an evil concept. It was now clear that the practical consequences of that outlook could only lead to disaster. What are the signs of our own time?

§52 Warnings of National Disaster

Now there were some present at that very season which told Jesus of the Galilæans, whose blood Pilate had mingled with their sacrifices. And he answered and said unto them,
Think ye that these Galilæans were sinners above all the Galilæans, because they have suffered these things? I tell you, Nay: but, except ye repent, ye shall all in like manner perish.

Or those eighteen, upon whom the tower in Siloam fell, and killed them, think ye that they were offenders above all the men that dwell in Jerusalem? I tell you, Nay: but, except ye repent, ye shall all likewise perish.

Galileans whose blood Pilate mingled with their sacrifices. The offence committed was obviously political since it was Pilate, the Roman Governor who had had them killed.

Ye shall all in like manner perish—at the hands of the Romans.

Except ye repent—unless those who hold the political concept of Christ's activity change their minds about the validity of that outlook. Repentance—an attitude which would open their minds to fresh insight.

Evidently the eighteen imprisoned in the Tower of Siloam were there for offences against Rome—insurrection.

Ye shall all likewise perish—as indeed they did forty years later when the patience and tolerance of the Romans gave out under repeated revolts, murders of Roman soldiers and sabotage. Jerusalem was destroyed and great numbers of its inhabitants slaughtered in AD 70 [21].

§53 Teaching About Reliance on Wealth

And one out of the multitude said unto Jesus, Teacher, bid my brother divide the inheritance with me. But Jesus said unto him, Man, who made me a judge or a divider over you?

And Jesus said unto them, Take heed, and keep yourselves from all covetousness: for a man's life consisteth not in the abundance of the things which he possesseth.

And Jesus spake a parable unto them, saying, The ground of a certain rich man brought forth plentifully: and he reasoned within himself, saying, What shall I do, because I have not where to bestow my fruits? And he said, This will I do: I will pull down my barns, and build greater; and there will I bestow all my corn and my goods. And I will say to my soul, Soul, thou hast much goods laid up for many years; take thine ease, eat, drink, be merry. But God said unto him, Thou foolish one, this night is thy soul required of thee; and the things which thou hast prepared, whose shall they be? So is he that layeth up treasure for himself, and is not rich toward God.

Lay not up for yourselves treasures upon the earth, where moth and rust doth consume, and where thieves break through and steal: but lay up for yourselves treasure in heaven, where neither moth nor rust doth consume, and where thieves do not break through nor steal: for where thy treasure is, there will thy heart be also.

A man's life consisteth not in the abundance of the things which he possesseth. The first expression of this insight we found in § 3 where Jesus said *Man shall not live by bread alone.* And since then, on a number of occasions and in a variety of forms of expression, Jesus has said that a man's life consists, most rewardingly, in complete obedience to the *Will of God*. (For the phrase *Will of God* read, what is true, good, right relative to each particular situation) [25].

So is he that layeth up treasure for himself and is not rich toward God. One becomes *rich toward God* by *minding the things of God* rather than *the things of men*. The method or process for becoming rich toward God is to *lose the life; deny the self*, § 35.

Where thy treasure is there will thy heart be also. So the nature of the treasure is the important thing. If your treasure is worldly goods, you will be preoccupied with guarding and extending that treasure. If your treasure is *fullness of life*, then you will be preoccupied with maintaining your awareness of and ready response to God's directing—the intimations of your moral sense.

§54 Saying on Light and Darkness

And when the multitudes were gathering together unto Jesus, he began to say,
The lamp of thy body is thine eye: when thine eye is single, thy whole body also is full of light; but when it is evil, thy body also is full of darkness.
Look therefore whether the light that is in thee be not darkness. If the light that is in thee be darkness, how great is the darkness!

This saying may be paraphrased as follows: *The lamp of your body is your will. When your will is committed to one thing (God's Will), you will be full of insight; but when your will is committed to many things (divided), you will experience no insight.* If on examination you find that what you supposed was right action has turned out to have been wrong, you may get back on the track by reaffirming your willingness to be controlled by *God's Will*—what is right in each situation. Maintaining the *Not my will but thine* attitude is difficult but essential and worth striving for.

§55 Limits of the Kingdom of God

And Jesus went on his way through cities and villages, teaching, and journeying on unto Jerusalem.
And one said unto him, Master, are they few that be saved?
And Jesus said unto them, Strive to enter in by the narrow door: for many, I say unto you, shall seek to enter in, and shall not be able.
Ye shall see Abraham, and Isaac, and Jacob, and all the prophets, in the kingdom of God, and yourselves cast forth without. And they shall come from the east and west, and from the north and south, and shall sit down in the kingdom of God.
And behold, there are last which shall be first, and there are first which shall be last.

As before, Jesus spent his day teaching.
Master are they few that be saved? Instead of answering this speculative question Jesus urged the man to save himself. *Sauve-qui-peut!* Never mind about anyone else. Just you strive to *enter in by the narrow door.* As Jesus saw the process for entering the Kingdom of God, it required just one

thing—the decision to do *the Will of God.* One does not have to decide what action would be *nice,* or *expedient* or *what would pay-off in one way or another,* but *only what is right.*

Shall not be able. Why not able? Because one cannot understand the process or cannot bring one's self to *lose one's life* or can no longer differentiate between right and wrong.

From the east and west and from the north and south—Jesus' confidence in the eventual wide acceptance of the condition for entrance into the Kingdom of God set neither geographical nor racial limits. This is a corrective to the belief of the religious leaders who held that only sons of Abraham were eligible.

For Christians, the world-wide spread of their religion is no doubt taken as evidence that Jesus' prediction was correct. However, it seems doubtful if that was what he had in mind.

§56 Forecast of his Death by Jesus

In that very hour there came certain Pharisees, saying to Jesus, Get thee out, and go hence: for Herod would fain kill thee. And he said unto them, Go and say to that fox, Behold, I must go on my way to-day and tomorrow, and the third day I am perfected: for it cannot be that a prophet perish out of Jerusalem.

Herod would fain kill thee. Herod would want to remove Jesus only if there was evidence that he had *gone political* and was leading an insurrection. At this stage it appears more likely that the Pharisees are fearful of what may happen to themselves if Jesus enters Jerusalem with the multitude of his followers.

The third day I am perfected. In three days he will be in Jerusalem. Jesus saw himself as a prophet and like all the prophets who had come to Jerusalem seeking to save the Jews from the consequences of one folly or another, he expected to be killed. Nevertheless, he intended to go through with his mission to warn the people against the *leaven of the Pharisees.*

§57 Teaching in Criticism of Anxiety

And Jesus said unto his disciples,
Be not anxious for your life, what ye shall eat, or what ye shall drink; nor yet for your body, what ye shall put on. Is not the life more than the food, and the body than the raiment?
Behold the birds of the heaven, that they sow not, neither do they reap, nor gather into barns; and God feedeth them. Are not ye of much more value than they?
And which of you by being anxious can add one cubit unto his stature?
And why are ye anxious concerning raiment? Consider the lilies of the field, how they grow; they toil not, neither do they spin: yet I say unto you, that even Solomon in all his glory was not arrayed like one of these. But if God doth so clothe the grass of the field which to-day is, and to-morrow is cast into the oven, shall he not much more clothe you, O ye of little faith?
Be not therefore anxious, saying, What shall we eat? or, What shall we drink? or, Wherewithal shall we

be clothed? For after all these things do the Gentiles seek.
Your Father knoweth that ye have need of all these things. Seek ye first his kingdom, and his righteousness; and all these things shall be added unto you.
Be not therefore anxious for the morrow: for the morrow will be anxious for itself. Sufficient unto the day is the evil thereof.

Jesus condemns anxiety as futile and argues, by analogy with the creatures of nature, that if man will but trust in God he will be taken care of as they are [25].

As elements in an ecological system, all living creatures get what they can take of Nature's bounty in competition with others. Those that can best cope, survive. In human society also, the more able do better for themselves; but anxiety is a fact of life whether one has much or little. Jesus' answer to the problem of anxiety is *Seek ye first his Kingdom and his righteousness and all these things (food, clothing, shelter) will be added unto you.* In what sense can this be true? [24, 25].

If a man gives priority to meeting the condition for entrance into the Kingdom of God, that is, commits himself unreservedly to doing the Will of God (responding to the guidance of his moral sense), he will experience a sense of wholeness, of security, of freedom from anxiety. He knows now who he is and what he wants to do and he knows that a dependable guide for action is available within himself at all times.

Relieved of the burden of anxiety, such a person

will be able to plan, anticipate problems and use what intelligence he has to make his way in a difficult, competitive world where most people are wandering blindly about and dying of self-inflicted wounds.

As more and more people meet the condition for becoming whole, integrated persons, human society must gradually change for the better. The tragedy is that nearly 2000 years after Jesus discovered *The Way*, so few people have ever heard of it.

§58 Teachings at the Table of a Pharisee

And it came to pass that Jesus went into the house of one of the rulers of the Pharisees on a sabbath to eat bread.
And he spake a parable unto those which were bidden, when he marked how they chose out the chief seats; saying unto them,
When thou art bidden of any man to a marriage feaSt, sit not down in the chief seat; leSt haply a more honourable man than thou be bidden of him, and he that bade thee and him shall come and say to thee, Give this man place. But when thou art bidden, go and sit down in the loweSt place; that when he that hath bidden thee cométh, he may say to thee, Friend, go up higher. For every one that exaltéth himself shall be humbled; and he that humbléth himself shall be exalted.
And he said to him also that had bidden him, When thou makeSt a dinner or a supper, call not thy friends, nor thy bréthren, nor thy kinsmen, nor rich neighbours; leSt haply they also bid thee again, and a recompense be made thee. But when thou makeSt a feaSt,

bid the poor, the maimed, the lame, the blind: and thou shalt be blessed; because they have not wherewith to recompense thee.

A person who exalts himself is *seeking to save his life*. This is the wrong process and leads to the undesired outcome—*loss of life*—in this case manifested as embarassment and frustration.

The recompense for inviting those who cannot invite back—poor, maimed, blind—will come from God. One will have a sense that one has done the right thing.

§59 The Costs of Discipleship

Now there went with Jesus great multitudes: and he turned, and said unto them,
If any man cometh unto me, and hateth not his own father, and mother, and wife, and children, and brethren, and sisters, yea, and his own life also, he cannot be my disciple.
For which of you, desiring to build a tower, doth not first sit down and count the cost, whether he have wherewith to complete it? Lest haply, when he hath laid a foundation, and is not able to finish, all that behold begin to mock him, saying, This man began to build, and was not able to finish.
Or what king, as he goeth to encounter another king in war, will not sit down first and take counsel whether he is able with ten thousand to meet him that cometh against him with twenty thousand? Or else, while the other is yet a great way off, he sendeth an ambassage, and asketh conditions of peace.

So therefore whosoever he be of you that renounceth not all that he hath, he cannot be my disciple. He that hath ears to hear, let him hear.

First sit down and count the cost . . . sit down first and take counsel. Jesus was against impulsive, emotional, ill-considered decisions to follow him. To make a sound decision one must know the facts, that is, what is meant by *deny himself, lose his life, renounce all that he hath.* So the first step is understanding.

If any man cometh after me and hateth not . . . Hateth is used here in the sense of renounce, cast-off, abandon. Obviously the Jewish family was very close knit (as it still is today), and thus *hateth father, mother, wife, children* was a way of indicating the necessity of detachment from traditional values. The loyalty which must be completely given is not to Jesus or even to his cause, but to God (the good, what is right in each situation).

In the discourse on the Kingdom of God, § 24, two of the parables portrayed man selling *all that he hath* to buy the treasure or the pearl. Since *all that he hath* must go, the most direct approach is to surrender control to God—that is, replace your own will (freedom to make choices) by God's Will —whatever is good, right in each situation. The motivation for doing this is the result—wholeness, fullness of life.

CHAPTER 12

Many Truths Taught in Parables

§60 Parables on the Worth of Sinners

Now all the publicans and sinners were drawing near unto Jesus for to hear him. And both the Pharisees and the scribes murmured, saying, This man receiveth sinners, and eateth with them.
And Jesus spake unto them these parables, saying,
¶ What man of you, having a hundred sheep, and having lost one of them, doth not leave the ninety and nine in the wilderness, and go after that which is lost, until he find it? And when he hath found it, he layeth it on his shoulders, rejoicing. And when he cometh home, he calleth together his friends and his neighbours, saying unto them, Rejoice with me, for I have found my sheep which was lost. I say unto you, that even so there shall be joy in heaven over one sinner that repenteth.
¶ Or what woman having ten pieces of silver, if she lose one piece, doth not light a lamp, and sweep the house, and seek diligently until she find it? And when she hath found it, she calleth together her friends and neighbours, saying, Rejoice with me, for I have found the piece which I had lost. Even so, I say unto you, there is joy in the presence of the angels of God over one sinner that repenteth.

¶ And he said, A certain man had two sons: and the younger of them said to his father, Father, give me the portion of thy substance that falleth to me. And he divided unto them his living. And not many days after the younger son gathered all together, and took his journey into a far country; and there he wasted his substance with riotous living. And when he had spent all, there arose a mighty famine in that country; and he began to be in want. And he went and joined himself to one of the citizens of that country; and he sent him into his fields to feed swine. And he would fain have been filled with the husks that the swine did eat: and no man gave unto him. But when he came to himself he said, How many hired servants of my father's have bread enough and to spare, and I perish here with hunger! I will arise and go to my father, and will say unto him, Father, I have sinned against heaven, and in thy sight: I am no more worthy to be called thy son: make me as one of thy hired servants. And he arose, and came to his father. But while he was yet afar off, his father saw him, and was moved with compassion, and ran, and fell on his neck, and kissed him. And the son said unto him, Father, I have sinned against heaven, and in thy sight: I am no more worthy to be called thy son. But the father said to his servants, Bring forth quickly the best robe, and put it on him; and put a ring on his hand, and shoes on his feet: and bring the fatted calf, and kill it, and let us eat, and make merry: for this my son was dead, and is alive again; he was lost, and is found. And they began to be merry. Now his elder son was in the field: and as he came and drew nigh to the house, he heard music and dancing. And he called to him one of the servants, and inquired what these things might be. And he said unto him, Thy brother is come; and thy father hath killed the fatted calf, because he hath received him safe and sound. But he was angry, and would not go in: and his father came out, and intreated him. But he answered and said to his father, Lo, these many years do I serve thee, and I never transgressed a commandment of thine: and yet thou never gavest me a kid, that I might make merry with my friends: but when this thy son came, which hath devoured thy living with harlots, thou killedst for him the fatted calf. And he said unto him, Son, thou art ever with me, and all that is mine is thine. But it was meet to make merry and be glad: for this thy brother was dead, and is alive again; and was lost, and is found.

For the religious leaders, the publicans (tax collectors) and sinners were altogether beyond the pale, religiously. For Jesus, according to these parables no line could be drawn. Those who were lost were just as valuable, potentially, as those who had never strayed. They needed only to be found. Jesus understood that to be his mission.

In the parable of the lost son, the younger son, *repentant*, said: *Father I have sinned against heaven and earth and in thy sight.* The older son asserted, *Thy son hath devoured thy living with harlots* i.e. *he is a sinner* which for him, was proper ground for excluding the younger man. However, for the father, what mattered was not the past act but the present attitude. Repentance is prerequisite to forgiveness.

The point Jesus was making in this parable was

that any person who sincerely repents of his sins will be forgiven and received back into normal relationship with God. This bypassed the whole sacrificial system of the time and, for that matter, the priest and the confessional of our time. In modern terms, if you are genuinely repentant, that is all that is necessary to get you back for a fresh start at responding to what your conscience is urging you to do. That old saying *Let your conscience be your guide,* though usually said facetiously, is sound advice.

§61 God *versus* Mammon

And Jesus said also unto the disciples, No servant can serve two masters: for either he will hate the one, and love the other; or else he will hold to one, and despise the other. Ye cannot serve God and mammon.
And the Pharisees, who were lovers of money, heard all these things; and they scoffed at Jesus. And he said unto them, Ye are they that justify yourselves in the sight of men; but God knoweth your hearts: for that which is exalted among men is an abomination in the sight of God.

Jesus says there are but two possible masters and these are mutually exclusive. If your master is to be God, you must be a full-time servant.

That which is exalted among men is an abomination in the sight of God. What is exalted by man? With what motivation? The contrast is self-direction vs. God-direction.

§62 Parable on the Futility of Duty

And Jesus said unto his disciples, Who is there of you, having a servant plowing or keeping sheep, that will say unto him, when he is come in from the field, Come straightway and sit down to meat; and will not rather say unto him, Make ready wherewith I may sup, and gird thyself, and serve me, till I have eaten and drunken; and afterward thou shalt eat and drink? Doth he thank the servant because he did the things that were commanded? Even so ye also, when ye shall have done all the things that are commanded you, say, We are unprofitable servants; we have done that which it was our duty to do.

In the time of Jesus, every aspect of the lives of the Jewish people was governed by the Law. It was the duty of each individual Jew to obey the Law in all its detail. No one received any credit for doing so but supposedly God was offended if one neglected any least part. But beyond the call of duty (the Law), Jesus says there is much more to be done. To be a *profitable servant* of God, the duty roster is not set by the requirements of conventional religion but by *every word that proceedeth out of the mouth of God* i.e. what one's moral sense offers as right action during every moment of one's waking day.

§63 Several Sayings of Jesus

¶ The law and the prophets were until John: from that time the gospel of the kingdom of God is preached, and every man entereth violently into it. But it is easier for heaven and earth to pass away, than for one tittle of the law to fall.

¶ Is it lawful on the sabbath day to do good, or to do harm? to save a life, or to kill? What man shall there be of you, that shall have one sheep, and if this fall into a pit on the sabbath day, will he not lay hold on it, and lift it out? How much then is a man of more value than a sheep! Wherefore it is lawful to do good on the sabbath day.

¶ He that is not with me is against me; and he that gathereth not with me scattereth.

¶ Beware of false prophets, which come to you in sheep's clothing, but inwardly are ravening wolves.

Before John, God—conceived of as King of the Jewish people—laid down the Law and commanded obedience to it. After John, Jesus discovered and taught that God was king only when individual man voluntarily accepted God's reign in his life. Hence for those who became subjects of God in this manner, the Law and the Prophets were no longer relevant. However, Jesus pointed out that the inherent conservatism of the religious leaders guaranteed that the Law would remain—that in fact their conservatism is such that *it is easier for heaven and earth to pass away than for one tittle of the Law to fall.* Has this tendency toward conservatism in religion made its appearance within the Christian Church? If so, what may be the psychological basis for this inflexibility?—this resistance to change?

According to the religious leaders, man could do on the Sabbath day only what was permitted in the Law. According to Jesus, man could do on the Sabbath day anything that was *good* and the individual could determine for himself what was good (right) for him to do on that day.

He that is not with me is against me. Either you are committed to doing God's will (what is good, right) or you are not. If you are so committed, you are *with* Jesus. If you are not so committed then you are against what Jesus stands for.

Beware of false prophets. Who were the false prophets of Jesus' time? Who are the false prophets of our own time?

§64 Parable on Deferred Judgement

And Jesus spake this parable; A certain man had a fig tree planted in his vineyard; and he came seeking fruit thereon, and found none. And he said unto the vinedresser, Behold, these three years I come seeking fruit on this fig tree, and find none: cut it down; why doth it also cumber the ground? And he answering saith unto him, Sir, let it alone this year also, till I shall dig about it, and manure it: and if it bear fruit thenceforth, well; but if not, thou shalt cut it down.

The householder was becoming impatient. Here Jesus had in mind the political situation—the increasing tension between the Roman rulers and the Jews resulting from repeated acts of violence and incipient insurrection. For the Romans, Judea was not a profitable colony—no fruit on that tree.

It was a warning. One day Rome would have had enough of that nonsense and put an end to it [21].

§65 Time of the Kingdom of God

And it came to pass, as Jesus was on the way to Jerusalem, that he was passing through the midst of Samaria and Galilee.
And being asked by the Pharisees, when the kingdom of God cometh, Jesus answered them and said, The kingdom of God cometh not with observation: neither shall they say, Lo, here! or, There! for lo, the kingdom of God is in the midst of you.
And he said unto them, Verily I say unto you, There be some here of them that stand by, which shall in no wise taste of death, till they see the kingdom of God come with power.

The Kingdom of God cometh not with observation. John believed that the Christ would come in a spectacular manner; destroy all evil and establish the Kingdom of God. Some of the Pharisees believed that the Christ would come as a political leader and drive out the Romans, thus clearing the way for the Kingdom of God. Jesus' statement here means that any watching for the coming of the Kingdom of God is futile.

The Kingdom of God is in the midst of you. Jesus' content for the phrase *Kingdom of God* was a kingdom composed of one or more voluntary subjects ruled by God. Thus even though there were no other subjects than Jesus himself it would still be true that the Kingdom of God already existed there in their midst. So the statement means that all expectations concerning a future arrival of the Christ to usher in the Kingdom of God are mistaken because the Kingdom of God is already here.

They shall see the Kingdom of God come with power. This statement says that Jesus was confident that many of his contemporaries would meet the condition for entrance into the Kingdom of God, § 55.

Jesus' position relative to the Christ concept is very clear here. If the sole function of the Christ as God's agent was to usher in the Kingdom of God then the concept was mistaken. Jesus got the Kingdom started all by himself—no destruction of the evil people; no war with the Romans; no bother, no fuss—except for the individual who aspires to enter. The cost of admission is high. *Every man entereth violently into it.*

§66 Parables on Importunity in Prayer

And Jesus spake a parable unto them to the end that they ought always to pray, and not to faint; saying, There was in a city a judge, which feared not God, and regarded not man: and there was a widow in that city; and she came oft unto him, saying, Do me justice of mine adversary. And he would not for a while: but afterward he said within himself, Though I fear not God, nor regard man; yet because this widow troubleth me, I will do her justice, lest she wear me out by her continual coming.

And Jesus said unto them, Which of you shall have a friend, and shall go unto him at midnight, and say to him, Friend, lend me three loaves; for a friend of mine is come to me from a journey, and I have nothing to set before him; and he from within shall answer and say, Trouble me not: the door is now shut, and my children are with me in bed; I cannot rise and give thee? I say unto you, Though he will not rise and give him, because he is his friend, yet because of his importunity he will arise and give him as many as he needeth.

Importunity, persistence is necessary in the one who prays if the prayer is to be answered. What one is seeking is insight—what is the right thing for me to do now? The answer must come from within one's self. On the one hand, nothing will come if one is ignorant of the facts and factors involved in the problem. On the other hand, however well informed one may be, nothing will come unless one maintains one's attitude of willingness to respond to the answer when it comes [25]. See § 87 for the supreme example of persistence.

§67 Several Sayings of Jesus

¶ Have faith in God. All things are possible to him that believeth. If ye have faith as a grain of mustard seed, ye would say unto this sycamine tree, Be thou rooted up, and be thou planted in the sea; and it would have obeyed you.
¶ A city set on a hill cannot be hid. Even so let your light shine before men, that they may see your good works, and glorify your Father.
¶ Give, and it shall be given unto you; good measure, pressed down, shaken together, running over. For

with what measure ye mete, it shall be measured unto you. Freely ye received, freely give.
⁋ Verily I say unto you, Inasmuch as ye did it unto one of these my brethren, even these least, ye did it unto me.

For *Faith* read *confidence in God*—i.e. confidence in one's moral sense—that it will indicate what is the right thing to do. Confidence also that insight will come if one persists and maintains the attitude of openness and willingness to act on what comes.

A religious person, after the manner of Jesus, is visible because, being a *good man*, his attitude and behaviour set him apart from others. A *good man* is a man totally committed to doing what is right, good in each situation.

With what measure ye mete it shall be measured unto you. This reciprocal process is inherent and automatic.

One of these, my brethren, even the least. Brethren here refers to others who, like Jesus, are in the Kingdom of God.

§68 Parable on the Basis of Justification

And Jesus spake also this parable unto certain which trusted in themselves that they were righteous, and set all others at nought:
Two men went up into the temple to pray; the one a Pharisee, and the other a publican. The Pharisee stood and prayed thus with himself, God, I thank thee, that I am not as the rest of men, extortioners, unjust,

adulterers, or even as this publican. I faſt twice in the week; I give tithes of all that I gĕt. But the publican, ſtanding afar off, would not lift up so much as his eyes unto heaven, but smote his breaſt, saying, God, be merciful to me a sinner.
I say unto you, This man went down to his house juſtified rather than the other.

God I thank thee that I am not as other men. Instead of taking the rest of mankind as the norm by which to determine your status, you might better take God (good) as your norm. When you do so you are immediately confronted with your shortcomings. The listing of virtues is a sure sign that you are *seeking to save your life.*

CHAPTER 13

Teaching and Journeying on to Jerusalem

§69 Teachings About Divorce

AND there came Pharisees unto Jesus, and asked him, Is it lawful for a man to put away his wife? And Jesus answered and said unto them, What did Moses command you? And they said, Moses suffered to write a bill of divorcement, and to put her away. But Jesus said unto them, For your hardness of heart he wrote you this commandment.
But from the beginning of the creation, Male and female made he them. For this cause shall a man leave his father and mother, and shall cleave to his wife; and the twain shall become one flesh: so that they are no more twain, but one flesh. What therefore God hath joined together, let not man put asunder.
¶And in the house the disciples asked Jesus again of this matter. And he saith unto them, Whosoever shall put away his wife, and marry another, committeth adultery: and if she herself shall put away her husband, and marry another, she committeth adultery.

This section has to do with divorce on grounds of adultery. Adultery is defined as a sexual relation between a married man and a woman other than his partner in the marriage.

In § 17, referring to Moses' law prohibiting adultery, Jesus said, *Anyone that looketh on a woman to lust after her committeth adultery with her already in his heart. And if thine eye causeth thee to stumble, pluck it out . . . and if thy hand causeth thee to stumble, cut it off . . .*

Why does Jesus feel so strongly about this matter? What consequence of lusting after someone could possibly justify such drastic corrective action as Jesus recommends? If a man lusts after his own wife does this carry the same or a lesser or no stigma?

Sexual intercourse has visceral effects which narrow and distort one's perception of reality. One's awareness is limited to the desired object. The same is true during sexual fantasy—simulated sexual intercourse. There is a reversion to the neuro-motor level of behaviour and at that level, there tends to be no concern for legality or other restraint. In that state, the conscience (*the Counsel of God*) is submerged. That is why Jesus felt so strongly about *lusting after.*

According to Moses, if one committed adultery one was in danger of God's judgment i.e. of being cast off, repudiated. But Jesus knew that sexual fantasy had that same outcome—one's awareness of *the Counsel of God* was greatly diminished if not entirely submerged. Thus to *look on a woman to lust after her* is, in its effect—*in the area that concerned Jesus*—equivalent to adultery.

Moses was aware that for large numbers of people, the animal-urge to copulate was stronger than the social pressure to abide by the commandment forbidding adultery. So, in support of those who respected the law and those whose marriage partners were adulterous, he required the adulterers to divorce their partners. This saved the law, did justice to the deserving and contributed to community stability.

Speaking privately with his disciples later, Jesus went on to say that if a man who had divorced his wife, remarried, he would thereby commit adultery. *In this context*, the reason for the divorce was that one partner to the marriage was engaging in sexual relations outside of the marriage. Jesus assumes that if that person marries again it will be to continue and facilitate his lustful activity. This will in effect be adultery for, as in the first instance, it will break his relationship with God—submerge his conscience.

It is important to see Jesus' ideal clearly. It was, that once a marriage has been consumated it becomes a life-long relationship. It is also important to see clearly that this ideal does not provide any basis whatever for statutory enactments having the purpose of forcing marriage partners to remain together throughout their life-times even though, for whatever reason, their relationship may have soured, long since. Nor does it mean that every person who has divorced or been divorced, for whatever reason, would necessarily offend God (submerge his conscience) if he marries again. It depends—every case is unique.

For Jesus, the moral quality of an action is

always relative to the person in his situation. Generalizing, laying down absolutes, coercing people, was quite foreign to the mind of Jesus. But foreign or not and to the shame of the institutions involved, Jesus' statements of ideals have been generalized and canon laws have been based upon them. Dreadful burdens have thereby been laid upon people and to a considerable extent these burdens remain.

§70 Relation of Possessions to Eternal Life

And as Jesus was going forth into the way, there ran one to him, and kneeled to him, and asked him, Good Teacher, what shall I do that I may inherit eternal life? And Jesus said unto him, Why callest thou me good? none is good save one, even God. Thou knowest the commandments, Do not kill, Do not commit adultery, Do not steal, Do not bear false witness, Do not defraud, Honour thy father and mother.
And he said unto him, Teacher, all these things have I observed from my youth. And Jesus looking upon him loved him, and said unto him, One thing thou lackest: go, sell whatsoever thou hast, and give to the poor, and thou shalt have treasure in heaven: and come, follow me. But his countenance fell at the saying, and he went away sorrowful: for he was one that had great possessions.
¶And Jesus looked round about, and saith unto his disciples, How hardly shall they that have riches enter into the kingdom of God! It is easier for a camel to go through a needle's eye, than for a rich man to enter into the kingdom of God.
And the disciples were amazed at his words. But Jesus

answereth again, and saith unto them, Children, how hard is it to enter into the kingdom of God!
¶ Peter began to say unto him, Lo, we have left all, and have followed thee. Jesus said, Verily I say unto you, There is no man that hath left house, or brethren, or sisters, or mother, or father, or wife, or children, or lands, but he shall receive a hundredfold now in this time, and shall inherit eternal life.

Why callest thou me good? None is good save one, even God. For Jesus, God was good but he felt that he himself was not good even though he was committed to doing what was good. Apparently he did not believe he was godly or perfect in any sense.

One thing thou lackest: go, sell whatsoever thou hast and give to the poor. One who possesses wealth is dependent on that wealth and is concerned to keep it for therein lies his security. So to tell a man to dispose of his wealth—to give it away, was as shocking an idea then as it is today. Did Jesus really mean it? See § 59.

One thing thou lackest. The response of the young man indicated that he was unwilling to pay the price—*life* was too expensive.

Children, how hard it is to enter into the Kingdom of God. It was hard then and no less so now because it involves a capitulation—a surrender of the freedom to choose one's own course of action in each situation. Instead, one must consciously decide *in advance* that one will always, henceforth, do what is right, the good thing—God's Will.

But no one will pay that price for nothing, and

no one is asked to do so. This is an offer—an offer of wholeness in exchange for obedience. An offer of fulfillment in exchange for complete and total obedience to the intimations of one's moral sense.

§71 Parable on the Basis of Reward

A householder went out early in the morning to hire labourers into his vineyard. And when he had agreed with the labourers for a denarius a day, he sent them into his vineyard. And he went out about the third hour, and saw others standing in the marketplace idle; and to them he said, Go ye also into the vineyard, and whatsoever is right I will give you. And they went their way. Again he went out about the sixth and the ninth hour, and did likewise. And about the eleventh hour he went out, and found others standing; and he saith unto them, Why stand ye here all the day idle? They say unto him, Because no man hath hired us. He saith unto them, Go ye also into the vineyard.

And when even was come, the owner of the vineyard saith unto his steward, Call the labourers, and pay them their hire, beginning from the last unto the first. And when they came that were hired about the eleventh hour, they received every man a denarius. And when the first came, they supposed that they would receive more; and they likewise received every man a denarius. And when they received it, they murmured against the householder, saying, These last have spent but one hour, and thou hast made them equal unto us, which have borne the burden of the day and the scorching heat. But he answered and said to one of them, Friend, I do thee no wrong: didst not thou agree with me for a denarius? Take up that which is thine, and go thy way; it is my will to give unto this last, even as unto thee.

The one thing that all the labourers had in common when they were hired was willingness to work. The reward was the same for all regardless of when they began working. In religious terms, when you decide to meet the condition—willingness to do the *Will of God*, you qualify for the reward, *life*—the same reward no matter when you meet the condition—that is, start to work.

This parable, if understood, would not be appreciated by the religious leaders. The suggestion that just anyone could qualify for the reward—membership in the Kingdom of God, if he were willing to *work*, starting now, would not go down well with those who expected not just special treatment but exclusive occupation by the sons of Abraham.

§72 Teaching on Standards of Greatness

And they were in the way, going up to Jerusalem; and Jesus was going before them: and they were amazed; and they that followed were afraid.
¶ And there come near unto him James and John, the sons of Zebedee, saying unto him, Teacher, we would that thou shouldest do for us whatsoever we shall ask of thee. And Jesus said unto them, What would ye that I should do for you? And they said unto him, Grant unto us that we may sit, one on thy right hand, and one on thy left hand, in thy kingdom.

But Jesus said unto them, Ye know not what ye ask. Are ye able to drink the cup that I drink? or to be baptized with the baptism that I am baptized with? And they said unto him, We are able. And Jesus said unto them, The cup that I drink ye shall drink; and with the baptism that I am baptized withal shall ye be baptized: but to sit on my right hand or on my left hand is not mine to give.
¶ And when the ten heard it, they began to be moved with indignation concerning James and John. And Jesus called them to him, and saith unto them, Ye know that they which are accounted to rule over the Gentiles lord it over them; and their great ones exercise authority over them. But it is not so among you: but whosoever would become great among you, shall be your minister: and whosoever would be first among you, shall be servant of all.
For whether is greater, he that sitteth at meat, or he that serveth? is not he that sitteth at meat? but I am in the midst of you as he that serveth.

The request of James and John *to sit one on thy right hand and one on thy left in thy kingdom* indicates that they still believed that Jesus was the Christ and that when they reached Jerusalem, the Kingdom of God would come into being—or at least, that Jesus, as Christ, would take over control. James and John wanted to be assured of good positions in the new regime.

Are you able to drink the cup that I drink or be baptised with the baptism that I am baptised with? The cup Jesus had in mind was his rejection by the religious leaders and the baptism, his anticipated death. As Jesus approached Jerusalem he showed increasing awareness of his now highly probable fate and he warned his disciples that their fate could very well be the same as his own.

Whosoever would become great among you shall be your minister and whosoever would be first among you shall be servant of all. Jesus did not condemn the ambition of the disciples for place and power but offered a sound procedure for its achievement. In saying *I am in the midst of you as he that serveth,* Jesus was pointing out that for himself personally, service was the normal expression of *life* already achieved.

By now it is obvious that *service* to others is not the process for achieving *life*—to suppose so is to confuse process and outcome. The sound process for achieving *greatness* is to serve people; the sound process for achieving *life* is to serve God— the good.

§73 The Rich Publican of Jericho

And Jesus entered and was passing through Jericho. And behold, a man called by name Zacchæus; and he was a chief publican, and he was rich. And he sought to see Jesus who he was; and could not for the crowd, because he was little of stature. And he ran on before, and climbed up into a sycomore tree to see him: for he was to pass that way.

And when Jesus came to the place, he looked up, and

said unto him, Zacchæus, make haste, and come down; for to-day I must abide at thy house. And he made haste, and came down, and received Jesus joyfully. And when they saw it, they all murmured, saying, He is gone in to lodge with a man that is a sinner.
And Zacchæus stood, and said unto the Master, Behold, Master, the half of my goods I give to the poor; and if I have wrongfully exacted aught of any man, I restore fourfold.
And Jesus said unto him, To-day is salvation come to this house, forasmuch as he also is a son of Abraham.

Jesus has been criticized for associating with sinners in § 10, § 20 and § 60. In § 10 he explained his association with the religious outcasts on the ground that they were sick and he knew the WAY to health. In § 20 he pointed out to the critical Pharisee that the woman (who came to him) had shown by her attitude that she was repentant and had faith—confidence in God. In § 60, Jesus said that it was normal for a person who had lost something valuable to search until he found it and then rejoice with his friends. The implication was that Jesus associated with sinners to the end that they might repent and return to God. Jesus was working to increase the number of God's subjects.

In this case in Jericho, Jesus' justification for associating with the publican was that *he also is a son of Abraham*—a Jew no less than were the Pharisees.

Salvation has come to this house. The attitude of Zacchaeus indicates a change of heart. No one becomes chief tax-collector and wealthy by consistently giving to the poor and restoring four-fold what he has stolen.

§74 Time of the Kingdom of God

And as they heard these things, Jesus added and spake a parable, because he was nigh to Jerusalem, and because they supposed that the kingdom of God was immediately to appear.
Jesus said therefore, A certain nobleman went into a far country. And he called ten servants of his, and gave them ten pounds, and said unto them, Trade ye herewith till I come. And it came to pass, when he was come back again, that he commanded these servants, unto whom he had given the money, to be called to him, that he might know what they had gained by trading. And the first came before him, saying, Sir, thy pound hath made ten pounds more. And he said unto him, Well done, thou good servant: because thou wast found faithful in a very little, have thou authority over ten cities. And the second came, saying, Thy pound, Sir, hath made five pounds. And he said unto him also, Be thou also over five cities. And another came, saying, Sir, behold, here is thy pound, which I kept laid up in a napkin: for I feared thee, because thou art an austere man: thou takest up that thou layedst not down, and reapest that thou didst not sow. He saith unto him, Out of thine own mouth will I judge thee. Thou knewest that I am an austere man, taking up that I laid not down, and reaping that I did not sow; then wherefore gavest thou not my money into the bank, and I, on my return, should have required it with

interest? And he said unto them that stood by, Take away from him the pound, and give it unto him that hath the ten pounds.
And when Jesus had thus spoken, he went on before, going up to Jerusalem.

It was the belief that the *Kingdom of God was immediately to appear* that sent the sons of Zebedee to Jesus to request a favour. Clearly, in spite of everything Jesus had said to the contrary, the disciples still expected him to assume the role of political leader when they reached Jerusalem.

The point of the parable here is that though different people have different gifts and capacities, each is responsible for the full use of what he has. Compare § 82 end for a similar thought. The relationship between the point of this parable and the historical situation is clear. Jesus' mind is on his probable death in Jerusalem. When he is gone it will be up to the disciples—*Unto you is given the mystery of the Kingdom of God*—to carry on with his mission of telling people the real meaning of God's Kingdom. Will they do it?

If the disciples fail to carry on after Jesus' death —and from what we have learned about them it seems doubtful that he could have had much confidence that they would, then his mission to show people the way to *life* and to save Jerusalem from destruction will have failed. His great discovery, the truth about the Kingdom of God will be lost— perish with him. A profound tragedy.

CHAPTER 14

Challenge of the Jerusalem Leaders by Jesus

§75 Jesus Enters Jerusalem as Popular Leader

AND as Jesus was now drawing nigh unto Jerusalem, even at the descent of the mount of Olives, the whole multitude of the disciples began to rejoice and praise God with a loud voice for all the mighty works which they had seen; saying, Blessed is he that cometh in the name of the Lord: peace in heaven, and glory in the highest.

And some of the Pharisees from the multitude said unto him, Teacher, rebuke thy disciples. And he answered and said, I tell you that, if these shall hold their peace, the stones will cry out.

And when Jesus drew nigh unto Jerusalem, he saw the city and wept over it, saying,

O Jerusalem, Jerusalem, which killeth the prophets, and stoneth them that are sent unto her! how often would I have gathered thy children together, even as a hen gathereth her chickens under her wings, and ye would not! Behold, your house is left unto you desolate, till ye shall say, Blessed is he that cometh in the name of the Lord.

If thou hadst known in this day, even thou, the things which belong unto peace! but now they are hid from thine eyes. For the days shall come upon thee, when thine enemies shall cast up a bank about thee, and compass thee round, and keep thee in on every side, and shall dash thee to the ground, and thy children within thee; and they shall not leave in thee one stone upon another; because thou knewest not the time of thy visitation.

And when Jesus was come into Jerusalem, all the city was stirred, saying, Who is this? And the multitudes said, This is the prophet, Jesus, from Nazareth of Galilee.

And he entered into Jerusalem, into the temple; and when he had looked round about upon all things, it being now eventide, he went out unto Bethany with the twelve.

Blessed is he that cometh in the name of the Lord. Earlier estimates of Jesus identified him with the Christ. Here he is hailed as a prophet. That Jesus should be greeted as a prophet is displeasing to the Pharisees because they have not only rejected him as of any religious significance but are planning to kill him.

The stones will cry out. If the people are silenced then inanimate Nature will announce that my message is from God.

Till they shall say, Blessed is he that cometh in the name of the Lord—until they acknowledge and accept the Prophets. Jesus' estimate of himself was, as we saw in § 26, that he was a Prophet.

The things that belong unto peace—in this historical situation, peace with Rome.

They shall not leave in thee one stone upon another. Jesus foresaw the destruction of Jerusalem and of the Temple as the outcome of the attitude of the Zealots and others toward Roman rule. For they believed that the Kingdom of God could not come until the rule of the Jewish state by Rome came to an end [21].

Because thou knewest not the time of thy visitation. From that visitation by the Prophet Jesus, the religious leaders and the people might have learned that the coming of the Kingdom of God required neither a political nor an apocalyptic Christ but rather a quiet internal change in the attitude of each individual. If they had learned this, the revolt against Rome need never have occurred.

This is the Prophet Jesus from Nazareth of Galilee. This was an estimate Jesus approved and one which mankind will eventually accept as his proper title.

§76 Jesus Casts Commerce from the Temple

And on the morrow they come to Jerusalem: and Jesus entered into the temple, and began to cast out them that sold and them that bought in the temple, and overthrew the tables of the money-changers, and the seats of them that sold the doves; and he would not suffer that any man should carry a vessel through the temple.
And Jesus taught, and said unto them, Is it not written, My house shall be called a house of prayer for all the nations? but ye have made it a den of robbers.

The Temple authorities probably obtained a considerable income for the temple or for themselves, by selling concessions to those who changed money and those who sold sacrificial animals. At the time of the Passover, people came to Jerusalem from all over the country and although Roman coinage was probably standardized, the availability of some facility for obtaining change would be convenient. But as now, moneychangers are sometimes short-changers and their charges tend to change.

Whatever Jesus may have hoped to achieve by his drastic action in the Temple, we may be sure that it was, for him, the right thing to do at the time. The inevitable result was still greater determination on the part of the religious authorities to remove him. But that probable outcome was not now the matter of primary concern for Jesus. His main concern was to save the Jewish people from destruction by the Romans and to that end he must arouse and convince them that they should reject the teaching of the religious leaders who by their non-cooperation with the Roman rulers were actually supporting the insurrection of the Zealots [21].

§77 Jesus Teaches in the Temple

And Jesus was teaching daily in the temple. But the chief priests and the scribes and the principal men of the people sought to destroy him, for they feared him. And they could not find what they might do; for the people all hung upon him, listening. For all the multitude was astonished at his teaching. And every evening he went forth out of the city to Bethany, and lodged there.

Aware of the increasing hostility of the authorities, Jesus went *all out* to get his message to the people—what the Kingdom of God was and what it was not. We have no report on what he actually said but it is clear from the reported reaction of the people who heard him that his message was fresh, different and very interesting, for it held the crowds and brought them back day after day.

The fear of the temple authorities is not surprising. A violent revolution was a possibility and not against Rome but against the religious leaders. Jesus' teaching on righteousness; on the Kingdom of God; his condemnation of the Scribes and Pharisees as hypocrites—if understood and taken up by the multitudes, could result in the repudiation of the religious leaders. But this does not happen without a leader and therefore the only way out for the religious leaders was to deprive the multitude of their leader, Jesus, before it was too late.

§78 Jewish Rulers Challenge Authority of Jesus

And they come again to Jerusalem: and as Jesus was teaching the people in the temple, there come to him the chief priests, and the scribes, and the elders; and they said unto him, Tell us: By what authority doest thou these things? or who gave thee this authority?
And Jesus said unto them, I will ask of you one question, and answer me, and I will tell you by what

authority I do these things. The baptism of John, was it from heaven, or from men? answer me.
And they reasoned with themselves, saying, If we shall say, From heaven; he will say, Why then did ye not believe him? But if we shall say, From men; all the people will stone us: for they be persuaded that John was a prophet.
And they answered Jesus and say, We know not. And Jesus saith unto them, Neither tell I you by what authority I do these things.

The request by the Jewish rulers for Jesus' *authority* for his action in the Temple has a bureaucratic ring to it. The *goings on* in the Temple had to be approved by the temple rulers who would give permission for some things but not for a radical teacher whose only authority was his own moral sense. Since the temple authorities refuse to evaluate John's baptism, it is obvious to Jesus that they are dishonest and hence there is no point in telling them of his *authority*.

§79 Parables in Condemnation of Jewish Leaders

And Jesus began to speak unto them in parables:
⁋A man had two sons; and he came to the first, and said, Son, go work to-day in the vineyard. And he answered and said, I will not: but afterward he repented himself, and went. And he came to the second, and said likewise. And he answered and said, I go, sir: and went not.
What think ye? Whether of the twain did the will of his father? They say, The first.

Jesus saith unto them, Verily I say unto you, that the publicans and the harlots go into the kingdom of God before you. For John came unto you in the way of righteousness, and ye believed him not: but the publicans and the harlots believed him: and ye, when ye saw it, did not even repent yourselves afterward, that ye might believe him.

¶ Hear another parable: There was a man that was a householder, which planted a vineyard, and set a hedge about it, and digged a pit for the winepress in it, and built a tower, and let it out to husbandmen, and went into another country. And at the season of the fruits he sent to the husbandmen a servant, that he might receive from the husbandmen of the fruits of the vineyard. And they took him, and beat him, and sent him away empty. And again he sent unto them another servant; and him they wounded in the head, and handled shamefully, and sent him away empty. And he sent another; and him they killed: and many others; beating some, and killing some. And the owner of the vineyard said, What shall I do? I will send my son: it may be they will reverence him. But when the husbandmen saw him, they reasoned one with another, saying, This is the heir: let us kill him, and take his inheritance. And they cast him forth out of the vineyard, and killed him. What therefore will the owner of the vineyard do unto them? He will come and destroy these husbandmen, and will give the vineyard unto others.

¶ And Jesus spake again a parable unto them, saying, A certain king made a marriage feast for his son, and sent forth his servants to call them that were bidden to the marriage feast: and they would not come. Again he sent forth other servants, saying, Tell them that are bidden, Behold, I have made ready my dinner: my oxen and my fatlings are killed, and all things are ready: come to the marriage feast. But they made light of it, and went their ways, one to his own farm, another to his merchandise. Then saith he to his servants, The wedding is ready, but they that were bidden were not worthy. Go ye therefore unto the partings of the highways, and as many as ye shall find, bid to the marriage feast. And those servants went out into the highways, and gathered together all as many as they found: and the wedding was filled with guests.

¶ And when the chief priests and the scribes and the Pharisees heard his parables, they perceived that he spake the parables against them. And when they sought to lay hold on him in that very hour, they feared the multitudes, because they took Jesus for a prophet.

The first story is a clear statement of what is required of an individual if he is to be religious after the manner of Jesus. Those in Jesus' audience, whether religious leaders or others, who answered the question understood quite well what was involved.

The publicans and harlots did not claim to be religious but they responded to John's call for righteousness. The religious leaders claimed to be religious but their response to John was to say that he was crazy—which they knew was not true.

The second story is the history of the treatment of the succession of prophets by the religious leaders of the Jews. Instead of listening to those who came to them *in the name of the Lord,* they rejected or killed them.

In the parable of the marriage feast, those who were expected to come (the religious leaders?), refused. So the feast (Jesus' teaching) was given to anyone who would come (listen). *They took Jesus for a prophet.* This was an estimate which Jesus could approve.

§80 Efforts to Accumulate Evidence Against Jesus

And they watched Jesus, and sent forth spies, which feigned themselves to be righteous, that they might take hold of his speech, so as to deliver him up to the rule and to the authority of the governor.

And when they were come, they say unto him, Teacher, we know that thou art true, and sayest and teachest rightly, and carest not for any one: for thou regardest not the person of men, but of a truth teachest the way of God. Tell us therefore, What thinkest thou? Is it lawful for us to give tribute unto Cæsar, or not? Shall we give, or shall we not give?

But Jesus perceived their craftiness, and said, Shew me the tribute money. And they brought unto him a denarius. And he saith unto them, Whose is this image and superscription? They say unto him, Cæsar's. Then saith he unto them, Render unto Cæsar the things that are Cæsar's; and unto God the things that are God's.

And they were not able to take hold of the saying before the people: and they marvelled at his answer, and held their peace.

¶And there came to Jesus certain of the Saducees,

they which say that there is no resurrection; and they asked him, saying, Teacher, Moses wrote unto us, that if a man's brother die, having a wife, and he be childless, his brother should take the wife, and raise up seed unto his brother. There were seven brethren: and the first took a wife, and died childless; and the second; and the third took her; and likewise the seven also left no children, and died. Afterward the woman also died. In the resurrection whose wife of them shall she be? for the seven had her to wife.

Jesus said unto them, Is it not for this cause that ye err, that ye know not the scriptures, nor the power of God? The sons of this world marry, and are given in marriage: but they that are accounted worthy to attain to that world, and the resurrection from the dead, neither marry, nor are given in marriage: for neither can they die any more: for they are equal unto the angels; and are sons of God, being sons of the resurrection.

But that the dead are raised, even Moses shewed when he calleth the Lord the God of Abraham, and the God of Isaac, and the God of Jacob. Now he is not the God of the dead, but of the living: for all live unto him. Ye do greatly err.

And when the multitudes heard it, they were astonished at his teaching.

⁋ And the scribes and the Pharisees bring a woman taken in adultery; and having set her in the midst, they say unto him, Teacher, this woman hath been taken in adultery, in the very act. Now in the law Moses commanded us to stone such: what then sayest thou of her?

CHALLENGE OF THE JERUSALEM LEADERS / 163

And this they said, trying him, that they might have whereof to accuse him.
But Jesus stooped down, and with his finger wrote on the ground. But when they continued asking him, he lifted up himself, and said unto them, He that is without sin among you, let him first cast a stone at her. And again he stooped down, and with his finger wrote on the ground. And they, when they heard it, went out one by one, beginning from the eldest, even unto the last: and Jesus was left alone, and the woman, where she was, in the midst. And Jesus lifted up himself, and said unto her, Woman, where are they? did no man condemn thee? And she said, No man, Master. And Jesus said, Neither do I condemn thee: go thy way; from henceforth sin no more.

¶ And one of the scribes came, and heard them questioning together, and knowing that Jesus had answered them well, asked him a question: Teacher, What commandment is the first of all?
Jesus answered, The first is, Hear, O Israel; The Lord our God, the Lord is one: and thou shalt love the Lord thy God with all thy heart, and with all thy soul, and with all thy mind, and with all thy strength. The second is this, Thou shalt love thy neighbour as thyself. There is none other commandment greater than these.
And the scribe said unto Jesus, Of a truth, Teacher, thou hast well said that he is one; and there is none other but he: and to love him with all the heart, and with all the understanding, and with all the strength, and to love his neighbour as himself, is much more than all whole burnt offerings and sacrifices.

And when Jesus saw that he answered discreetly, he said unto him, Thou art not far from the kingdom of God.
And no man after that durst ask Jesus any question.

The Jewish leaders conspired to get Jesus into the hands of the Roman Governor who, having power of life and death over the Jews could order his execution.

Is it lawful to give tribute to Caesar or not? Obviously the Roman tax law, effective in Judea at the time, required that taxes be paid. However, since Judaism was a Theocracy, God being head of the state, to pay the tax and thus recognize another head of state, was to be disloyal to God. Note that though *Should we pay or should we not pay?* was a religious question, the answer could have political implications.

If Jesus had advised refusal to pay tribute to Rome, he could be regarded as a political enemy of Rome. Had he advised the payment of the tax, he could be charged by the Jews with disloyalty to God. A dilemma. How does Jesus handle it?

Jesus' solution to that problem was *Render unto Caesar the things that are Caesar's and to God the things that are God's.* This negated the validity of the theocratic concept of the Jewish state and the validity of the concept of the Christ as a political leader required to drive out the Romans. No need to drive out the Romans if paying taxes was not a sign of disloyalty to God i.e. did not alter the basic premise that man's individual allegiance is to God as King. Loyalty to God as king is not dependent upon the forms of political control of the nation, nor is it limited by national boundaries.

Jesus met the specific problem raised by the Sadducees about life after death by asserting that the resurrection was not physical—no body. At the same time he undertakes to establish confidence in the notion of *some* form of life after death, which the Sadducees did not believe in, by quoting from Moses—an authority for them.

God is not the God of the dead but of the living. Stripped of its context, this makes sense. The *living* are, according to Jesus, those who love God with their whole being. The *dead* are those who do not. The *living* are those who do the *Will of God*—follow the *straightened way*. The *dead* are those who follow the *broad way*.

Is it not for this cause that ye err, that ye know not the scriptures nor the power of God? The scriptures represented accumulated human wisdom: the power of God was the power of goodness, right action. If a man had no knowledge of the one nor experience of the other, he would be unlikely to have much insight on any basic religious problem.

He that is without sin among you, let him cast the first stone. Since no one cast a stone, presumably all were at least honest enough to admit to themselves that they were not qualified to do any stoning. Their own guilt made them ineligible to implement the law of Moses concerning adultery.

Neither do I condemn thee: go thy way; from

henceforth sin no more. Clearly Jesus regarded adultery as a sin, but he, being conscious of his own imperfections, could not condemn the woman for being a sinner. The past is past: it is your present attitude toward God that is important.

Thou shalt love the Lord thy God . . . Thou shalt love thy neighbor as thy self. One is to love God with the whole personality and one is to love one's neighbor as much as one loves one's self. Loving, caring for one's self is encouraged. Selfishness is not condemned. But one must be impartial. The neighbor is to receive equal treatment. Since the word *love* has currently a number of meanings [19], perhaps we ought to examine our use of it to see which meaning is implied.

Loving God (truth, goodness, rightness) cannot be equated to a feeling or emotion. In any case, feelings and emotions cannot be commanded. They are not under the control of the will. In the saying, love is commanded, action is required. Thus loving, caring for, is not a passive sentiment but an active, outgoing action.

It should be noted that the loving of your neighbor as your self is an outcome of loving God with your whole personality; but loving God with your whole personality is not an outcome of loving your neighbor as yourself. For if you love God with your whole personality, you gain *life*. Loving your neighbor as yourself does not lead to *life* but does lead to satisfactory social relationships.

To love God . . . to love his neighbor as himself is much more than all whole burnt offerings and sacrifices. One could also say that it is much more in its outcome than may be obtained by believing that Jesus was the Christ.

Thou art not far from the Kingdom of God. The attitude of the Scribe was one of appreciation of Jesus' insight and he acknowledged that these two laws were of supreme importance. He understood the process for entrance into the Kingdom of God. Only one thing more was needed—to take the step.

It is interesting to recall three stages in the development of Western man's understanding of what is involved in being religious.

About 600 BC, Moses' code of laws appeared—(1) Deut, 5: 10-21. Its purpose was to regulate the life and religious practices of the Hebrews. In the form of commandments, supposedly spoken by God directly to Moses, these laws listed acts forbidden under threat of punishment if they were broken and promise of prosperity if they were kept. In Deut. 6:5 we find an additional commandment—*Thou shalt love the Lord thy God with all thy heart and with all thy soul and with all thy strength and with all thy mind.*

Something over 600 years later, we find reported in (1) Lk. 10: 25-28,—*A certain lawyer questioned Jesus, saying, What shall I do to inherit eternal life?* Jesus asked him what he found in the Scriptures bearing on that problem. The lawyer replied: *Thou shalt love the Lord thy God with all thy heart and with all thy soul and with all thy strength and with all thy mind—AND THY*

NEIGHBOR AS THYSELF. And Jesus said, Thou hast answered right, this do and thou shalt live. (This incident was considered in § 44.) The addition (1) Lev. 19:18 shown capitalized above, is an important supplement to Deut. 6:5. Neighbors are unavoidable!

In § 80 above, a Scribe asks Jesus: *What commandment is first of all?* Jesus answered, *The first is Hear O Israel, The Lord our God, the Lord is One: and thou shalt love the Lord thy God with all thy heart and with all thy soul and with all thy mind and with all thy strength: the second is Thou shalt love thy neighbor as thy self. There is none other commandment greater than these. And the scribe said unto Jesus, Of a truth, Teacher, thou hast well said he is one and there is none other than he, and to love him with all the heart and with all the understanding and with all the strength, and to love his neighbor as himself is much more than all whole burnt offerings and sacrifices. And Jesus said unto him, Thou art not far from the Kingdom of God.*

Note (a): in § 44, the lawyer did not quote Moses' laws but gave as the important Scripture, love of God and love of neighbor.

(b): In § 80, Jesus said that no other commandment (e.g. none of Moses' commandments), was greater than that which commanded love of God and love of neighbor.

(c): In § 80, the Scribe not only does not dispute Jesus' claim in note (b), but volunteers the opinion that love of God and love of neighbor are more efficacious than the whole Temple sacrificial cultus.

These were of course individual insights. For the religious authorities, Moses' statutes and his status as a law-giver were unchallenged.

In § 19, Jesus says that *all the Prophets and the Law prophesied until John.* He is here referring to the insight he gained when he was baptised by John, namely, that *if one is wholly committed to do God's will,* (what is right in each situation), *one comes to know what action is right for oneself.* This eliminated the need for all external codes of conduct as e.g. Moses' Laws. This was surely the greatest advance of all, but it was not a discovery that the law-makers and religious leaders were likely to greet with enthusiasm. Even now, after 2500 years, Moses' Ten Commandments are not only current but are the very foundation of our religious and legal institutions.

The next advance in man's understanding of the meaning of religion has come from the work of Scientists—physiologists and micro-biologists— who have advanced our knowledge of the evolutionary process, especially as it relates to man. See [25] and (11, 12).

CHAPTER 15

Discourse in Condemnation of Scribes and Pharisees

§81 Discourse in Condemnation of Scribes and Pharisees

THEN spake Jesus to the multitudes and to his disciples, saying, Beware of the scribes, which desire to walk in long robes: they make broad their phylacteries, and enlarge the borders of their garments. They love the chief place at feasts, and the chief seats in the synagogues, and the salutations in the marketplaces. They devour widows' houses, even while for a pretence they make long prayers. All their works they do for to be seen of men.

They love to be called of men, Rabbi. But be not ye called Rabbi: for one is your teacher, and all ye are brethren. Neither be ye called Master: for one is your master. And call no man your father on the earth: for one is your Father.

Whosoever shall exalt himself shall be humbled; and whosoever shall humble himself shall be exalted. He that is greatest among you shall be your minister.

¶ Woe unto you, scribes and Pharisees, hypocrites! for ye lade men with burdens grievous to be borne, and ye yourselves touch not the burdens with one of your fingers.

Woe unto you, scribes and Pharisees, hypocrites! because ye shut the kingdom of God against men: for ye enter not in yourselves, neither suffer ye them that are entering in to enter.

Woe unto you, scribes and Pharisees, hypocrites! for ye compass sea and land to make one proselyte; and when he is become so, ye make him twofold more a son of hell than yourselves.

Woe unto you, ye blind guides, which say, Whosoever shall swear by the temple, it is nothing; but whosoever shall swear by the gold of the temple, he is bound by his oath. Ye fools and blind: for whether is greater, the gold, or the temple that hath sanctified the gold? And, Whosoever shall swear by the altar, it is nothing; but whosoever shall swear by the gift that is upon it, he is bound by his oath. Ye blind: for whether is greater, the gift, or the altar that sanctifieth the gift?

Woe unto you, scribes and Pharisees, hypocrites! for ye tithe mint and anise and cummin, and have left undone the weightier matters of the law, justice, and mercy, and integrity. Ye blind guides, which strain out the gnat, and swallow the camel.

Woe unto you, scribes and Pharisees, hypocrites! for ye cleanse the outside of the cup and of the platter, but within they are full from extortion and excess. Thou blind Pharisee, cleanse first the inside of the cup and of the platter, that the outside thereof may become clean also.

Woe unto you, scribes and Pharisees, hypocrites! for ye are like unto whited sepulchres, which outwardly appear beautiful, but inwardly are full of dead men's bones, and of all uncleanness. Ye outwardly appear righteous unto men, but inwardly ye are full of hypocrisy and iniquity.

Woe unto you, scribes and Pharisees, hypocrites! for ye build the sepulchres of the prophets, and garnish the tombs of the righteous, and say, If we had been in the days of our fathers, we should not have been partakers with them in the blood of the prophets. Wherefore ye witness to yourselves, that ye are sons of them that slew the prophets. Fill ye up then the measure of your fathers.

¶And the scribes and the Pharisees began to press upon Jesus vehemently, and to provoke him to speak of many things; laying wait for him, to catch something out of his mouth.

All their works they do to be seen of men. In § 17, Jesus suggested that the truly religious person will do his righteousness in secret and look to God for commendation.

One is your Teacher . . . One is your Master . . . One is your Father. For Jesus, the one who was teacher, master and father was God. Recall § 2—*This day have I begotten thee.*

Whosoever shall exalt himself shall be humbled and whosoever shall humble himself shall be exalted. The most complete act of self-humbling is that given by Jesus in the Paradox—*Whosoever shall lose his life shall save it.* § 35 The self-humbling process is *lose one's life.*

He that is greatest among you shall be your minister. More commonly, he that is powerful enough to command service is rated greatest.

Jesus reserved his most severe denunciation of the Scribes and Pharisees until he reached Jerusalem. If he had spoken earlier he might have been arrested before he reached the city and many days of teaching the multitudes along the way would have been lost. Also, Jerusalem and the Temple were the centre, so to speak, of their religion and there would be very large numbers of people from all over the country there for the occasion of the Passover. What he had to say about the religious leaders would have its largest audience and make its greatest impact if spoken there. Thus Jerusalem at Passover was the best choice of time and place for this denunciation.

Whether or not one commends Jesus for this devastating criticism of the religious leaders depends on one's grasp of the political situation at the time. Because of their mistaken conception of how the Kingdom of God was to come and their preoccupation with the minutia of religious observance, the religious leaders were apparently quite unaware of the revolt that was brewing, of its probable consequences for the Jewish people. As a result of the same blindness and refusal to learn anything new, their fathers had killed the prophets of their day rather than listen and learn from them.

Fill up the measure of your fathers. In effect, your predecessors killed the prophets rather than heed what they had to say. Go ahead and do the same to me. They did.

Laying wait for him to catch something out

of his mouth. What they wanted to hear was something which they could report to the Roman Governor. If Jesus said something which could be construed as inimical to Roman interests, then the Jewish leaders could have him removed without having his death blamed on themselves.

CHAPTER 16

Discourse on Events of the Future

§82 Discourse on Events of the Future

AND as Jesus went forth out of the temple, one of his disciples saith unto him, Teacher, behold, what manner of stones and what manner of buildings!
And Jesus said unto him, Seest thou these great buildings? there shall not be left here one stone upon another, which shall not be thrown down.
⁋And as Jesus sat on the mount of Olives over against the temple, Peter and James and John and Andrew asked him privately, Tell us, when shall these things be? and what shall be the sign when these things are about to be accomplished?
⁋And Jesus began to say unto them, When ye shall hear of wars and rumours of wars, be not troubled: these things must needs come to pass. For nation shall rise against nation, and kingdom against kingdom: there shall be famines and pestilences. These things are the beginning of travail: but the end is not yet.
⁋But when ye see the abomination of desolation standing where he ought not (let him that readeth understand), then let them that are in Judæa flee unto the mountains. And let them that are in the midst of

Jerusalem depart out. And let not them that are in the country enter therein. For these are days of vengeance. Woe unto them that are with child and to them that give suck in those days! And pray ye that your flight be not in the winter. For those days shall be tribulation, such as there hath not been the like from the beginning of the creation which God created until now, and never shall be.

¶ Now from the fig tree learn her parable: when her branch is now become tender, and putteth forth its leaves, ye know that the summer is nigh. Verily I say unto you, This generation shall not pass away, until all these things be accomplished.

¶ The days will come, when ye shall desire to see the Day of the Son of man, and ye shall not see it. And they shall say to you, Lo, there! Lo, here! go not away nor follow after them.

Take heed that no man lead you astray. For many shall come, saying, I am the Christ; and, The time is at hand. They shall lead many astray. Go ye not after them.

¶ For as the lightning, when it
    lighteneth out of the one part under the heaven,
    shineth unto the other part under heaven;
so shall the Son of man be in his Day.
As it came to pass in the days of Noah,
even so shall it be also in the Day of the Son of man.
    They ate, they drank, they married, they were given
    in marriage, until the day that Noah entered into
    the ark, and the flood came, and destroyed them all.
Likewise even as it came to pass in the days of Lot;
    They ate, they drank, they bought, they sold, they

planted, they builded; but in the day that Lot went out from Sodom it rained fire and brimstone from heaven, and destroyed them all.
After the same manner shall it be in the Day that the Son of man is revealed.
In that day,
> he which shall be on the housetop,
> and his goods in the house, let him not go down to take them away: and let
> him that is in the field
> likewise not return back.

In that night
> there shall be two men on one bed;
> > the one shall be taken, and the other shall be left:
> there shall be two women grinding together;
> > the one shall be taken, and the other shall be left.

⁋ And they answering say unto Jesus,
> Where, Master?

And Jesus said unto them,
> Where the carcase is, thither will the vultures also be gathered together.

⁋ But of that Day knoweth no one, not even the angels in heaven, neither the Son, but the Father.
Take ye heed: for ye know not when the time is.
It is as when ten virgins took their lamps, and went forth to meet the bridegroom. And five of them were foolish, and five were wise. For the foolish, when they took their lamps, took no oil with them: but the wise took oil in their vessels with their lamps. Now while the bridegroom tarried, they all slumbered and slept. But at midnight there is a cry, Behold, the bridegroom! Come ye forth to meet him. Then all those virgins

arose, and trimmed their lamps. And the foolish said unto the wise, Give us of your oil; for our lamps are going out. But the wise answered, saying, Peradventure there will not be enough for us and you: go ye rather to them that sell, and buy for yourselves. And while they went away to buy, the bridegroom came.

¶ Take ye heed to yourselves: for they shall deliver you up to councils; and in synagogues shall ye be beaten; and before governors and kings shall ye stand. It shall turn unto you for a testimony.

And when they lead you to judgement, and deliver you up, be not anxious beforehand what ye shall speak: but whatsoever shall be given you in that hour, that speak ye. For it is not ye that speak, but the Spirit of your Father that speaketh in you.

And brother shall deliver up brother to death, and the father his child; and children shall rise up against parents, and cause them to be put to death. And ye shall be hated of all men. In your patience ye shall win your lives.

Behold, I send you forth as sheep in the midst of wolves: be ye therefore wise as serpents, and harmless as doves.

A disciple is not above his teacher. It is enough for the disciple that he be as his teacher. If they have called the master of the house Beelzebub, how much more shall they call them of his household!

There is nothing covered up, that shall not be revealed: and hid, that shall not be known. What I tell you in the darkness, speak ye in the light: and what ye hear in the ear, proclaim upon the housetops.

And I say unto you my friends, Be not afraid of them

which kill the body, and after that have no more that they can do. Are not five sparrows sold for two farthings? and not one of them is forgotten in the sight of God. But the very hairs of your head are all numbered. Fear not: ye are of more value than many sparrows.
Every one who shall confess me before men, him will I also confess before my Father. But whosoever shall deny me before men, him will I also deny before my Father. He that heareth you heareth me; and he that rejecteth you rejecteth me; and he that rejecteth me rejecteth him that sent me.

¶ For it is as when a man, going into another country, called his own servants, and delivered unto them his goods. And unto one he gave five talents, and to another two, to another one; to each according to his several ability; and he went on his journey.
Straightway he that received the five talents went and traded with them, and made other five talents. In like manner he also that received the two gained other two. But he that received the one went away and digged in the earth, and hid his master's money.
Now after a long time the master of those servants cometh, and maketh a reckoning with them.
And he that received the five talents came and brought other five talents, saying, Sir, thou deliveredst unto me five talents: lo, I have gained other five talents. His master said unto him, Well done, good and faithful servant: thou hast been faithful over a few things, I will set thee over many things.
And he also that received the two talents came and said, Sir, thou deliveredst unto me two talents: lo, I

have gained other two talents. His master said unto him, Well done, good and faithful servant; thou hast been faithful over a few things, I will set thee over many things.
And he also that had received the one talent came and said, Sir, I knew thee that thou art a hard man, reaping where thou didst not sow, and gathering where thou didst not scatter: and I was afraid, and went away and hid thy talent in the earth: lo, thou hast thine own. But his master answered and said unto him, Thou wicked and slothful servant, thou knewest that I reap where I sowed not, and gather where I did not scatter; thou oughtest therefore to have put my money to the bankers, and at my coming I should have received back mine own with interest.
Take ye away therefore the talent from him, and give it unto him that hath the ten talents.
To whomsoever much is given, of him shall much be required.

Tell us, when shall these things be? And what shall be the sign? The theme of this discourse is the time when the attack on Jerusalem and the destruction of the Temple will take place. There is no other reference. The prophesy was fulfilled in AD 70.

But the end is not yet—the end of the tolerance of the Romans for the incessant agitation by Zealots against Roman occupation.

The abomination of desolation refers to the presence in the Temple of the Roman Standard (flag) symbolizing Roman rule. For the Jews there was only one ruler, God, and for the symbol of another ruler to be lodged in God's holy place (the Temple), was the extreme of desecration.

For those days shall be tribulation such as there hath not been the like from the beginning of Creation which God created until now and never shall be. For the details of the siege and destruction of Jerusalem by the Romans see [21], (19), (24).

Evidence of Jesus' awareness of and concern about the political situation is revealed in a number of places as e.g. § 51, *Signs of the Times;* § 52, *the Galileans whose blood Pilate mingled with their sacrifices;* § 64, *the Parable of Deferred Judgment;* § 75, *Jesus' lament: If thou hadst known in this day, even thou, the things that belong unto peace!;* § 80, the issue of state taxation by Rome—*Is it lawful to give tribute to Caesar or not? Shall we give or shall we not give?* § 82, Jesus' sketch of the probable fate of Jerusalem; *When ye see the abomination of desolation standing where he ought not . . . then let them that are in Judaea flee unto the mountains . . . for these are days of vengeance.* And finally, § 91, as Jesus is being led to his execution: He said, *Daughters of Jerusalem, weep not for me but weep for yourselves and for your children.*

"What was likely to be the fate of Jesus' disciples and of the movement initiated by him in this revolutionary situation? That was a major concern of Jesus during his latter days. And prominent among his fears was the possible influence of those men who from time-to-time appeared claiming to be the Messiah, National Deliverers, and appealing to the sword on behalf of the national hope" (25). That there was frequent occurrence of such messianic claimants, both before and during the life of Jesus, is shown by a report in The Acts of the Apostles (27). The dire fate of the men who associated themselves with these *false-christs* shows why Jesus warned his disciples against them.

"The menace of the Zealot military leadership [21] associated with Messianic claimants consisted not only in its danger to the life of the nation but also in its threat to the right understanding of the relation between state and religion, i.e. between Caesar and God" (25). If Jesus' position relative to tax payment, § 80, were generally understood and accepted, the motivation for the Zealot revolt would be undercut and discredited. It was thus vital that the disciples continue teaching what Jesus had taught them about the manner of the coming of the Kingdom of God.

While Jesus was alive, the disciples were unlikely to be led astray by *false-christs* for they believed that Jesus was that expected political-leader. *They had hoped that it was he who would redeem Israel . . . They had supposed that the Kingdom of God was immediately to appear.* But what would be their orientation after Jesus was gone; when the armed revolt had failed and disaster threatened? What resource would then remain to them other than hope of direct intervention by God? And that compulsive hope for an intervention could now be satisfied only with its apocalyptic form. To subscribe to that belief and become absorbed in the expectation of an imminent judgment and catastrophic destruction could be as distracting to their teaching mission as had their earlier belief.

In anticipation of this development, Jesus offers the apocalyptic solution—only to take it away again. *The days will come when ye shall desire to see the Day of the Son of Man . . . but ye shall not see it.* See [20] end.

They will not see it because of its nature—it will come *as the lightning*—unpredictable, all over in a flash. No point in *watching* for the Coming. And instead of the apocalyptic messiah they had heard about from John who would come as a judge and destroyer of evil, the Son of Man will select—*one will be taken and the other left.* Taken where? *Where the body is there will the vultures be gathered together* i.e. to a place appropriate to its essential nature. Thus the *Day of the Son of Man* was the end of the Age—the time when each man will be assigned to his ultimate destiny. There will be no point in *waiting* for the Coming—it will come when it comes and the outcome will be what it will be. Only God knows when it will come but as the parable of the Virgins shows, those who are wise will prepare themselves for a long wait. The Coming of the Son of Man is not imminent. This was a corrective for those who might otherwise seek to evade their proper responsibility for action—teaching what

Jesus had taught them about the Kingdom of God —by waiting for God to intervene.

This presentation of the Day by Jesus was calculated to remove the apocalyptic hope as effectively as Jesus' death would remove the political hope. As Jesus knew from § 3 on, God was a non-intervenor and the messianic concept was a product of wishful thinking—a fantasy. But psychologically, the disciples needed to believe in an intervention and so Jesus gave them one—a safe one! If now the disciples accept Jesus' concept of this ultimate intervention, to the exclusion of all others, they could escape becoming victims of the armed conflict which Jesus expected to sweep the country within the life-time of his followers. And if they spend their time teaching what Jesus has taught them concerning the nature of the Kingdom of God, they could even reduce the armed conflict by depriving the Zealots and others of their basic motivation for fighting Rome. It was a gamble—a desperate solution by a desperate man. As history shows, it did not avail but it was worth a try.

Ye shall be hated by all men. This would result if the disciples taught what they had supposedly learned from Jesus for his message was divisive— the new wine would destroy the old wine-skins and those who peddled it would be attacked.

Be not afraid of them which kill the body and after that have no more that they can do. This was Jesus' attitude toward his enemies but one must wonder whether Jesus imagined that the disciples would have what it would take to face that challenge.

Jesus tried to encourage his disciples but in addition to encouragement, he reminds them that they have a responsibility. He has taught them all they could learn and now, *to whom much is given, of him shall much be required.* But nothing whatever is to be expected toward the advancement of the Kingdom of God from people who, fearful of the future, always seek to protect themselves.

§83 Teaching by Jesus in Jerusalem

And every day Jesus was teaching in the temple; and every night he went out, and lodged in the mount that is called the mount of Olives. And all the people came early in the morning to him in the temple, to hear him.

Jesus evidently made use of all the time available to him to teach and his audience was eager to hear what he had to say.

CHAPTER 17

Final Hours of Jesus with His Disciples

§84 Conspiracy for the Arrest of Jesus

Now after two days was the feast of the passover and the unleavened bread. And the chief priests and the scribes sought how they might take Jesus with subtilty, and kill him. But they said, Not during the feast, lest haply there shall be a tumult of the people. And Judas Iscariot, he that was one of the twelve, went away unto the chief priests, that he might deliver Jesus unto them. And they, when they heard it, were glad, and promised to give him money. And he sought how he might conveniently deliver Jesus unto them in the absence of the multitude.

. . . *Sought how they might take him with subtlety.* In the beginning the religious leaders charged Jesus with blasphemy and with breaking the Law i.e. they tried to discredit him as a religious teacher. Then they tried to obtain evidence that he was fomenting rebellion against Rome—in an effort to have the Roman Governor act against Jesus. These efforts having failed, they now propose direct action—get hold of the man and then invent charges against him.

During the final days of his teaching in the Temple, Jesus was protected from his enemies by the interest and responsiveness of the multitude. Hence the need for *subtlety* if this radical teacher was to be removed without danger to the Jewish leaders themselves.

§85 The Passover with the Disciples

And the day of unleavened bread came, on which the passover must be sacrificed. And Jesus sent Peter and John, saying, Go and make ready for us the passover, that we may eat. And they said unto him, Where wilt thou that we make ready? And Jesus said, Go into the city to such a man, and say unto him, The Teacher saith, My time is at hand; I keep the passover at thy house with my disciples. And the disciples did as Jesus appointed them; and they made ready the passover.

And when the hour was come, Jesus sat down, and the twelve with him. And he said unto them,

With desire I have desired to eat this passover with you before I suffer: for I say unto you, I will not eat it, until it be fulfilled in the kingdom of God.

And he received a cup, and when he had given thanks, he said, Take this, and divide it among yourselves: for I say unto you, I will not drink from henceforth of the fruit of the vine, until that day when I drink it new in the kingdom of God.

Behold, the hand of him that betrayeth me is with me on the table. And they began to question among themselves, which of them it was that should do this thing.

With desire I have desired to eat this Passover with you. Although Jesus had hoped to share the Passover meal with his disciples, *he did not do so.* This is not surprising considering not only his imminent death but the failure of his effort to arouse the people to an appreciation of the peril that lay ahead. And it must have been very clear to him as he faced death that from the point of view of the future of his missionary effort, the disciples would contribute little. Whether or not he could have averted the tragedy of the destruction of Jerusalem had he lived cannot be known but the certainty was that his followers would not affect that outcome. A bitter cup indeed!

Until that day when I drink it new in the Kingdom of God. This is rather obscure but seems to suggest that Jesus believed his relationship with God would not terminate with his death.

§86 Withdrawal to the Mount of Olives

And when they had sung a hymn, they went out unto the mount of Olives. And Jesus saith unto them, All ye shall be offended: for it is written, I will smite the shepherd, and the sheep shall be scattered abroad. But Peter said unto him, Although all shall be offended, yet will not I. And Jesus saith unto him, Verily I say unto thee, that thou to-day, even this night, before the cock crow, shalt deny me. But he spake exceeding vehemently, If I must die with thee, I will not deny thee. And in like manner also said they all.

Peter had more than once revealed his lack of understanding and of those elementary insights which a person of even his limited capacity might have had, had he chosen the *straight and narrow way*. But it may be that he never understood what all the talk was about. He was certain that Jesus was the Christ and that was enough for him. Jesus' forecast of Peter's future behaviour was accurate.

§87 At the Place Named Gethsemane

And they come unto a place which was named Gethsemane: and Jesus saith unto his disciples, Sit ye here, while I pray. And he taketh with him Peter and James and John, and began to be greatly agitated, and sore troubled. And he saith unto them, My soul is exceeding sorrowful even unto death: abide ye here, and watch.

And Jesus went forward a little, and fell on the ground, and prayed that, if it were possible, the hour might pass away from him. And he said, Abba, Father, all things are possible unto thee; remove this cup from me: howbeit not what I will, but what thou wilt.

And he cometh, and findeth them sleeping, and saith unto Peter, Simon, sleepest thou? couldest thou not watch one hour? Watch and pray, that ye enter not into temptation: the spirit indeed is willing, but the flesh is weak.

And again Jesus went away, and prayed, saying, O my Father, if this cannot pass away, except I drink it, thy will be done. And again he came, and found them sleeping, for their eyes were very heavy; and they wist not what to answer him.

And Jesus left them again, and went away, and prayed

a third time, saying again the same words. Then cometh he to the disciples, and saith unto them, Sleep on now, and take your rest: it is enough: the hour is at hand. Arise, let us be going: behold, he is at hand that betrayeth me.

It was obvious to Jesus that he had reached the end of the road. His enemies were closing in on him assisted by one of his own group. What he had done up to that point had been right for him, even though it had led to this seemingly terminal situation. He did not want to die—no healthy, normal, human being does and he, even less than any for, given time, he believed that he could save his people from destruction.

It is clear here that Jesus had no intention of doing anything other than the Will of God. It is equally clear that he had no thought or expectation that God would intervene to save him—that possibility had been dismissed at the outset of his publc career, § 3. His agonized effort here must have been a persistent search for new insight. *Ask, seek, knock—importune.* What is the right thing to do now? He could flee or remain and die. In either case he would have failed in his mission. Surely God would show him another way—some new insight would come to him. He must continue to ask and wait for an answer. But time ran out. In the end, events determined what he must do. A new situation and a fresh quest. What is the Will of God for me in this new situation?

§88   Betrayal and Arrest of Jesus

And straightway, while Jesus yet spake, cometh Judas, one of the twelve, and with him a multitude with swords and staves, from the chief priests and the scribes and the elders.

Now he that betrayed Jesus had given them a token, saying, Whomsoever I shall kiss, that is he; take him, and lead him away safely. And when he was come, straightway Judas came to him, and saith, Rabbi; and kissed him. And they laid hands on Jesus, and took him.

And behold, one of them that were with Jesus stretched out his hand, and drew his sword, and smote the servant of the high priest. Then saith Jesus unto him, Put up again thy sword into its place: for all they that take the sword shall perish with the sword.

And Jesus said unto the chief priests, and captains of the temple, and elders, which were come against him, Are ye come out, as against a robber, with swords and staves? When I was daily with you in the temple, ye stretched not forth your hands against me: but this is your hour, and the power of darkness.

Then all the disciples left Jesus, and fled.

Take him and lead him away safely. There was a chance that if the multitude to which Jesus had spoken daily in the Temple, had heard of his arrest, there would have been an attempt made to rescue him. Hence the need for precautions.

All that take the sword shall perish by the sword. This observation has been fully endorsed, not only by the destruction of Jerusalem, but by 1900 years of history since that time.

When I was daily in the Temple ye stretched not forth your hands against me—for the very good reason that the multitude was on Jesus' side.

This is your hour and the power of darkness. The power of darkness vs. the power of light; evil vs. good; evil people determined to kill a good man.

CHAPTER 18

Judicial Trials and Crucifixion of Jesus

§89 The Trial Before the Jewish Authorities

AND they seized Jesus, and led him away, and brought him into the high priest's house. But Peter followed afar off. And when they had kindled a fire in the midst of the court, and had sat down together, Peter sat in the midst of them. And a certain maid seeing him as he sat in the light of the fire, and looking stedfastly upon him, said, This man also was with Jesus. But he denied, saying, Woman, I know him not. And after a little while another saw him, and said, Thou also art one of them. But Peter said, Man, I am not. And after the space of about one hour another confidently affirmed, saying, Of a truth this man also was with Jesus: for he is a Galilæan. But Peter said, Man, I know not what thou sayest. And the Master turned, and looked upon Peter. And Peter remembered the word of the Master, how that he said unto him, Before the cock crow this day, thou shalt deny me. And he went out, and wept bitterly. And the men that held Jesus mocked him, and beat him. And they blindfolded him, and asked him, saying, Prophesy: who is he that struck thee? And many other things spake they against him, reviling him.

And as soon as it was day, the assembly of the elders of the people was gathered together, both chief priests and scribes; and they led Jesus away into their council. Now the chief priests and the whole council sought witness against Jesus to put him to death; and found it not. For many bare false witness against him, and their witness agreed not together. And there stood up certain, and bare false witness against him, saying, We heard him say, I will destroy this temple that is made with hands, and in three days I will build another made without hands. And not even so did their witness agree together.

And the high priest stood up in the midst, and asked Jesus, saying, Answerest thou nothing? what is it which these witness against thee? But Jesus held his peace, and answered nothing.

Again the high priest asked Jesus, and saith unto him, If thou art the Christ, tell us. But he said unto them, If I tell you, ye will not believe: and if I ask you, ye will not answer. And they all said, Art thou the Son of God? And Jesus said unto them, Ye say that I am. And they said, What further need have we of witness? for we ourselves have heard from his own mouth. And they all condemned him to be worthy of death.

When identified as one of Jesus' followers, Peter, fearful that he also would be seized and put to death, denied any knowledge of Jesus. From Jesus' prediction, here confirmed, it is clear that he had no illusions about the character of this disciple. Having fled with the other disciples when Jesus was arrested, why did Peter come to Jesus' trial where he was almost certain to be identified? Could it be that even at this extremity, Peter expected Jesus to announce himself as the Christ; switch roles with his gaolers and emerge triumphantly?

The story of the witness concerning the destruction of the Temple and its re-building was no doubt a garbled account of Jesus' prediction that the Temple would be destroyed by the Romans.

If thou art the Christ, tell us. To which Jesus replied: *If I tell you ye will not believe and if I ask you, ye will not answer.* Much earlier Jesus had said, § 24: *Give not that which is holy unto the dogs, neither cast your pearls before the swine, lest haply they trample them under their feet, and turn and rend you.* No point in trying to explain your way of life to people whose only interest is in your death.

Art thou the Son of God? is the same question as before—*Art thou the Christ?* Jesus' answer—*Ye say that I am.* i.e. *You are saying that I am making that claim.* But there is no evidence anywhere up to this point, in the material considered, that Jesus ever made such a claim for himself. On the contrary, he consistently denied that he was the Christ.

§90 The Trial Before the Roman Authorities

And the whole company of them rose up, and brought Jesus before Pilate the governor. And they began to accuse him, saying, We found this man perverting our nation, and forbidding to give tribute to Cæsar, and saying that he himself is Christ a king. And Pilate asked him, saying, Art thou the King of the Jews? And Jesus answered him and said, Thou sayest. And the chief priests accused him of many things. And Pilate again asked him, saying, Answerest thou nothing? behold how many things they accuse thee of. But Jesus no more answered anything; insomuch that Pilate marvelled.

And Pilate said unto the chief priests, I find no fault in this man. But they were the more urgent, saying, He stirreth up the people, teaching throughout all Judæa, and beginning from Galilee even unto this place. But when Pilate heard it, he asked whether the man were a Galilæan. And when he knew that he was of Herod's jurisdiction, he sent him unto Herod, who himself also was at Jerusalem in these days.

Now when Herod saw Jesus, he was exceeding glad: for he was of a long time desirous to see him, because he had heard concerning him. And he questioned him in many words; but Jesus answered him nothing. And the chief priests and the scribes stood, vehemently accusing him. And Herod with his soldiers set him at nought, and mocked him, and arraying him in gorgeous apparel sent him back to Pilate.

And Pilate called together the chief priests and the rulers, and said unto them, Ye brought unto me this man, as one that perverteth the people: and behold, I, having examined him before you, found no fault in this man touching those things whereof ye accuse him: no, nor yet Herod: for he sent him back unto us; and behold, nothing worthy of death hath been done by him. I will therefore chastise him and release him.

Now at the feast Pilate the governor used to release unto them one prisoner, whom they asked of him. And the multitude went up and began to ask him to do as he was wont to do unto them. And Pilate answered them, saying, Will ye that I release unto you the King of the Jews? For he perceived that for envy the chief priests had delivered him up.

And there was one called Barabbas, a notable prisoner, lying bound in prison with them that had made insurrection, men who in the insurrection had committed murder.

And the chief priests stirred up the multitude, that he should rather release Barabbas unto them. And they cried out all together, saying, Away with this man, and release unto us Barabbas. And Pilate again answered and said unto them, What then shall I do unto him whom ye call the King of the Jews? And they cried out, Crucify him. And Pilate said unto them, Why, what evil hath he done? I have found no cause of death in him: I will therefore chastise him and release him. But they cried out exceedingly, Crucify, crucify him.

And their voices prevailed. And Pilate gave sentence that what they asked for should be done. And he released him that for insurrection and murder had been cast into prison, whom they asked for; but Jesus he delivered up to their will.

And the soldiers led Jesus away within the court, which is the Prætorium; and they call together the whole band. And they clothe him with purple, and plaiting a crown of thorns, they put it on him; and they began to salute him, Hail, King of the Jews! And they smote his head with a reed, and did spit upon him. And when they had mocked him, they took off from him the purple, and put on him his garments. And they lead him out to crucify him.

We found this man perverting our nation. In fact there was no basis for their charge of perversion. There was a basis for asserting that Jesus was undermining their authority by showing that they were fundamentally wrong in both their religious and their social outlook and practice.

We found this man forbidding to give tribute to Caesar. Jesus' position was actually just the opposite, namely, *Render unto Caesar the things that are Caesar's.*

We found this man saying that he himself is Christ, a King. This again was contrary to fact. Jesus had made repeated efforts to correct those who expressed the belief that he was the Christ.

Jesus answered Pilate and said, thou sayest. This is the same reply as in § 89—*Ye say that I am.* In both places this seems to mean, My accusers say that I am, but I am not making any such claim.

Jesus no more answered anything. There was no point in saying anything else since his accusers had their minds made up and Pilate was not interested.

And Pilate said unto the Chief Priests, I find no fault in this man. If Jesus had claimed before Pilate that he was indeed the King of the Jews, Pilate would have shown interest at once and would have found this a real fault in Jesus for such a claim would have had serious political implications. Since Pilate found *no fault* in Jesus, the *thou sayest* from Jesus must have had, for Pilate, the meaning of a denial.

He stirreth up the people . . . to this place. The religious authorities intended Pilate to understand that Jesus was a political agitator and that he was inciting people all over the country to revolt against Roman occupation. Actually the stirring up of the people of which Jesus was guilty was against the political implications of the belief about the future held by the religious leaders.

When Herod questioned him, Jesus made no reply. There was no way to explain to the Roman Tetrarch what moved him to take the action he had taken.

Neither Pilate nor Herod found anything in Jesus' behaviour which carried important political implications. From their findings therefore there was no way that Jesus could be identified with the contemporary political concept of the Christ.

Pilate's offer to chastise Jesus and then release him was intended to placate the Jewish rulers who had demanded that Jesus be punished for his behaviour.

When the mob which the religious leaders had gathered together was asked to choose between the folk-hero Barabbas who was in prison for revolt against Roman rule, and Jesus, who had openly stated that Roman taxes should be paid, their choice was obvious. Barabbas was set free.

Pilate's question, *What then shall I do unto him*

whom ye call King of the Jews? indicates that he did not think much of the charge preferred by the Jewish rulers.

§91   The Crucifixion of Jesus

And when they led Jesus away, they laid hold upon one Simon of Cyrene, coming from the country, and laid on him the cross, to bear it after Jesus.
And there followed Jesus a great multitude of the people, and of women who bewailed and lamented him. But Jesus turning unto them said, Daughters of Jerusalem, weep not for me, but weep for yourselves, and for your children. For behold, the days are coming, in which they shall say, Blessed are the barren, and the wombs that never bare, and the breasts that never gave suck. Then shall they begin to say to the mountains, Fall on us; and to the hills, Cover us. For if they do these things in the green tree, what shall be done in the dry?
And they bring Jesus unto the place Golgotha, which is, being interpreted, The place of a skull. And they offered him wine mingled with myrrh: but he received it not. And they part his garments among them, casting lots upon them, what each should take. And it was the third hour, and they crucified him. And with him they crucify two robbers; one on his right hand, and one on his left. And the superscription of his accusation was written and set up over his head: THE KING OF THE JEWS. And they sat and watched him there.
And Jesus said, Father, forgive them; for they know not what they do.

And they that passed by railed on him, wagging their heads, and saying, Ha! thou that deŝtroyeŝt the temple, and buildeŝt it in three days, save thyself, and come down from the cross. In like manner also the chief prieŝts mocking him among themselves with the scribes said, He saved others; himself he cannot save. Lêt the Chriŝt, the King of Israel, now come down from the cross, that we may see and believe. He truŝtêth on God; lêt him deliver him now, if he desirêth him.

And it was now about the ninth hour. And when Jesus had cried with a loud voice, he said, Father, into thy hands I commend my spirit: and having said this, he yielded up his spirit.

And when the centurion, which ŝtood by over againŝt Jesus, saw what was done, he said, Certainly this was a righteous man.

For behold the days are coming . . . Jesus again refers to what he sees to be the fate of the Jews and Jerusalem which will result from the attitude of the Jewish leaders toward Roman rule.

For if they do these things in the green tree, what will be done in the dry? If in a time of relative political calm they (the Roman rulers) will put a good man to death purely on the ground of political expediency, even though they have found him to be entirely innocent of any political wrong doing, what will they do when the present minor incidents have given way to open revolt and general insurrection?

Since Jesus was apparently the only one who

saw the eventual outcome of the attitude of the Jewish leaders and had gone *all-out* to warn the mass of the people against following the lead of those *blind guides,* his removal from the scene made that catastrophe all but inevitable.

And Jesus said, Father, forgive them, for they know not what they do. This attitude of forgiveness even of those who are killing him is consistent with Jesus' teaching throughout his brief public career. Since he had become wholly God's man, neither the fear of death nor hate for his executioners was present in his consciousness during his final hours. It is an example—indeed the supreme example—of the *fruit* of a *good* man.

* *

PART II

INFORMATION SUPPLEMENTARY TO PART I AND SOME REFLECTIONS ON JESUS' TEACHING

CHAPTER 19

Dictionary Definitions of Some Words Used in this Book (16)

By Permission from Webster's Third International Dictionary © 1976 by G. and C. Merriam Co., Publishers of the Merriam-Webster Dictionaries.
Note: Some of the definitions are abbreviations of those given in Webster—the part chosen being that which is most relevant to the use of the word in the text.
1) *Aware* 2b: showing heightened perception and ready comprehension and appreciation, informed, knowing, alert.
2) *Conscience* 1a: the sense of right or wrong within the individual . . . the awareness of the moral goodness or blameworthiness of one's own conduct, intention, or character together with a feeling of obligation to do or be that which is recognized as good, often felt to be instrumental in producing feelings of guilt or remorse for ill-doing.
3) *Emotion* 1c: a physiological departure from homeostasis that is subjectively experienced in strong feeling (as of love, hate, desire or fear) and manifests itself in neuromuscular, respiratory, cardiovascular, hormonal, and other bodily changes preparatory to overt acts which may or may not be performed.

4) *Forgive* 1: to cease to feel resentment against on account of wrong committed: to give up claim to requital from or retribution upon (an offender).
5) *Homeostasis* 1: tendency toward maintenance of a relatively stable internal environment in the bodies of higher animals through a series of interacting physiological processes (as the maintenance of a fairly constant degree of body heat in the face of a widely varying external temperature).
2: tendency toward maintenance of a relatively stable psychological condition of the individual with respect to contending drives, motivations and other psychodynamic forces.
6) *Moral Sense* 1: feeling of the rightness or wrongness of an action or the ability to have such feelings.
7) *Repent* 1: to turn from sin out of penitence for past wrongdoings, abandon sinful or unworthy purposes and values, and dedicate oneself to the amendment of one's life.
8) *Right* 1: an ethical or moral quality that constitutes the ideal of moral propriety . . . : something morally just or consonant with the light of nature: the straight course.
9) *Righteous* 1: doing that which is right: acting rightly or justly: conforming to the standard of the divine or the moral law: free from guilt or sin.

Supplementary definition
of the word Conscience:

Although not so defined in Webster, Conscience may be equated with the phrases: Word of

God, Counsel of God, Will of God, Holy Ghost, Spirit of the Lord. All these phrases represent the efforts of people to put into words that urge to do what one conceives to be right, good. They were all coined by people who thought of God as a person. For Jesus, conscience was the voice of Abba, Father; for Socrates it was a *friendly spirit*—his daemon, which had been with him from childhood. It told him when a proposed action was wrong. For Paul of Tarsus, it was Christ—*Christ liveth in me.* For Emmanuel Kant, it was *Thou Shalt*—the categorical imperative. For the poet Francis Thompson, it was *the Hound of Heaven.* For animals generally, conscience is the injunction to act—to move or not to move in response to stimuli from the environment. The development of consciousness in man does not involve a break with the inherited integrated neuro-motor system but does involve *an extension of the information base for the injunction to right action.*

Redefinition of some words used by Jesus.

There are a number of words in Jesus' vocabulary which are rather obscure in meaning or have been so prostituted as to require rehabilitation or replacement. For example:
Faith: The faith of the primitive Christian community was based on the belief that the crucified Jesus had been resurrected and raised up and that he would return soon to act as judge of men. See [23, second part]. And because the disciples had believed that Jesus was the Christ before he was killed, they were convinced that when he came

again they as believers would receive preferred treatment. So the message to those they hoped to win to their *faith* was: Believe that Jesus was the Christ and you will be saved from destruction when he returns as judge of righteousness.

Three hundred years later when the events of the weeks following Jesus' death were now legend and the Christian community was Gentile rather than Jewish, the Christian Faith had become purely a matter of belief. Belief in one God could be taken for granted when the Christians had a Jewish background. Not so now. So the Nicene Creed (credo, I believe), Eastern Church, circa AD 325, read (10): "I believe in one God, the Father Almighty, maker of Heaven and Earth and of all things visible and invisible, and in one Lord Jesus Christ." To this was added, in the 9th century, "and in the Holy Ghost." During the long period of Christian history many creeds have been formulated. All call for the acceptance of certain propositions regarded by the particular sect as a necessary minimum commitment before an outsider is admitted into fellowship with the group.

The word *faith* as used by Jesus does not require a willingness to subscribe to something for which no satisfactory evidence has been offered. This does seem to be its connotation as used by some Christian sects. Rather, as Jesus used the word (see § 9, 18, 20, 25, 57, 67), Faith means having confidence in God—that is, confidence in the dependability of one's own moral sense and a ready willingness to respond to it [25].

Love: Whatever this word may have meant to Jesus, its present meanings seem to be: a) a sentimental attachment to a person or thing; b) an emotional state as in *I am in love* or, c) more commonly these days, *making love*—sexual intercourse. A substitute phrase is *to care for*. In any case action in a concrete situation is implied. If one cares for a person, one must do something for that person. If one cares for (loves) God (the Good, what is right), one must be totally committed to seeking out and doing what one perceives to be right in each situation.

Sin: In Judaism, sin was any deviation in action from obedience to God's Law. Among Christians, Roman Catholicism has its own definition of sin as in fact do many of the protestant sects.

In modern terms, sin is the failure to act upon the intimations of one's moral sense—the ignoring of the urging of one's conscience to act in a certain way. One experiences a sense of guilt due to the fact that one has neglected or denied one's most basic element—one's guide to right action. Sin is a violation of one's integrity, one's wholeness.

Forgiveness: Since no god is offended, none need be placated. One forgives oneself. One acknowledges to one's self, honestly, that one has done wrong. One then reaffirms one's commitment to *the good*. It is the present intention that is important. See § 80. For forgiveness of others, see [19] above.

CHAPTER 20

Judaism in Jesus' Time. (10, 13, 29).

At the time of Jesus, Judaism was a revealed religion setting forth the natures of God and Man and the proper relationship between them. The Law, which required man's obedience, was composed of those written regulations which Moses supposedly received from God together with a host of customs and traditional practices inherited from the remote past. It was the duty of the individual Jew to obey every detail of the Law, written and unwritten. There was no system of credits for good performance but every deviation, however trivial, received condemnation as a sin. The remedy for sin—to obtain God's forgiveness—involved propitiation, expiation and repentance. This procedure was spelled out clearly enough. However, it was recognized that the Temple cultus would be effective in obtaining forgiveness only if the petitioner were sincere in his repentance.

Much of the ceremonial Law was related to the Temple—the cult of sacrifices, the various offerings and how they were to be made. All of this was in the hands of the priesthood which performed these ceremonies according to its own traditions.

In the Gospels there are frequent references to the Scribes and the Pharisees. These were religious sects which were identified socially with the middle class.

The *Scribes* were learned in the Law, both written and unwritten. They acted as the interpreters of the Law and spelled out the details of its observance so that the individual Jew might know what was required of him. Some of the Scribes were Pharisees.

The *Pharisees* were distinguished by their strict adherence to the Law, especially to the traditional religious practices . . . They assumed the task of instructing the common people in the Law and set an example of its observance by their faithful attention to its details.

The *Sadducees* were not a religious sect but a social class. The wealthy families among the laity together with the upper level of the priesthood were represented in this group. They disagreed with the Pharisees on a number of matters as e.g. the Law. For the Saducess, the Law was what Moses brought. If Moses had not brought it, it was not valid. Thus the ancient customs and the Traditions of the Elders were not taken seriously by the Sadducees. Further, they found nothing in the Scriptures to support the belief of the Pharisees in a resurrection of the body and life after death. For the Sadducees this was just pharisaic fantasy. The Christian position on these matters obviously derived from the Pharisees. It is worth while to pause for a while to consider the influence these myths have had on the development of Western civilization and culture.

The Messiah (Christ) Concept.

"The idea of a Messiah, a Redeemer, sent by God, is common among different peoples throughout history and may reflect a universal psychological pattern" (10).

Among the Jews, the most ancient form of this concept was the Day of Jehovah or the Day of the Lord. The thought was that Jehovah would himself intervene—on his day. The later version of this belief was that Jehovah would not come himself but would send a human agent—the Son of Man.

At the time of Jesus the belief was that the coming of a Messiah was imminent. But there was controversy as to the function of this divine agent. Some held that he would be a political leader who would bring about the expulsion of the Roman rulers and restore the autonomy of the Jewish state. See [23, first part]. Others expected a Messiah who would impose a righteous order on the Jewish people. See [23, second part].

In Hebrew, the word Messiah meant God's Anointed. In Greek this became Christos; in Latin, Christus and in English, Christ. The word Christ will be used for Messiah in this book.

CHAPTER 21

Revolts of the Jews Against Rome, AD 6 to AD 73

The fundamental reason for the revolts was that the rule of Rome, including the payment of taxes, implied that Caesar was King. This contradicted the belief of the Jews that God was their King. Loyalty to God seemed to require disloyalty to Rome. The Messianic Hope in its political form supported those who rejected collaboration with Rome.

There were a number of religious sects and political parties among the Jews and these were not necessarily in agreement on basic issues.

Galilee was the home of the revolutionary movement. *The Zealots*, tenacious in their opposition to alien rule, rejected any form of collaboration with Rome. The national expectation that a Christ would come as a political leader played an important role in motivating the revolutionaries. The Zealots had some supporters among the *Scribes and Pharisees* but most members of these sects were moderates politically, and though they did not cooperate fully with the Roman rulers, they joined with the high priesthood and other prominent men in Jerusalem in a futile effort to restrain the rebels. In general, their outlook on the future was that the Christ would come when all the Jews were keeping the Law—as they themselves claimed to be doing.

The *Sadducees* were the ESTABLISHMENT—a party of wealth, a closed circle of aristocratic families including the high priesthood. They could have said (misquoting Pogo), "We have seen the future and it is us." They collaborated fully with the Roman rulers and thus preserved their rights and privileges.

The *Herodians*, supporters of Herod's regime and dynasty were with the Sadducees in these matters.

Recall Jesus' position relative to the Messianic Hope, the Zealot movement and the manner of the coming of the Kingdom of God. In § 3, Jesus rejected the Political Messiah concept as evil and in § 80 he made it clear that he did not share the view that loyalty to God required refusal to collaborate with the Roman rulers. In § 51 and § 52, we found a clear indication of Jesus' position relative to the acts of the freedom-fighters. In § 64, the eventual outcome of the Zealot inspired disturbances is foreseen. In § 82, the attack on and destruction of Jerusalem is visualized and described in an effort to forewarn the disciples and to ensure their faithful adherence to their assigned task— teaching about the Kingdom of God. That was of vital importance for if Jesus' conception of how the Kingdom of God was to come were well understood and accepted, the revolutionary movement would be undermined and discredited.

There were three revolts against the Romans, all Zealot led. The revolt in AD 6 was suppressed by Herod the King, and that in AD 36 by Pilate but the revolutionary movement was not destroyed. An open revolt broke out in Galilee in AD 66. At first the insurgents had some success but superior Roman forces under the command of Vespasian brought most of Palestine under control by AD 68. "In AD 70, the conflict between the Jewish people and Rome reached its climax; Jerusalem was sacked and destroyed; the Temple burned; the inhabitants slain or sold into slavery. This was the tragic end of many decades of clash between two fundamentally opposed cultures. Jesus lived and taught in the mid-period between the early conflicts and this ultimate collision between Jewish religion and nationalism and Roman paganism and empire" (25).

Even after the fall of Jerusalem there were pockets of resistance. The last of these, the fortress Masada, held out for three years and then all its defenders died in a mass-suicide—a final gesture of defiance to Rome. For a full account of the war and the details of the siege of Jerusalem, see (19) and (24).

CHAPTER 22

The Effect of Emotional Arousal On Moral Discrimination

According to Moses, acts of murder and adultery were offensive to God but hate was proper toward a non-Jew, § 17. Jesus had the insight that what was offensive to God (defiled a man), was something which preceded these overt acts, namely the thoughts and fantasies involving anger, hate, sexual desire etc, § 30.

The words anger, hate, revenge, lust all symbolize or are suggestive of emotional states which are reflex responses to certain stimuli presented by our environment. The visceral changes which accompany these reactions may well have contributed to individual and/or species survival during the long evolutionary development of man and animals generally. Such reactions are therefore *natural* though in the social milieu of modern life they are often quite inappropriate.

Our question here is: In what sense is it true that these emotional reactions break one's relationship with God, that is, affect the functioning of one's moral sense or one's response to it? What do we now know about the physiological and psychological effects of emotions that throws light on this problem?

First, some definitions [19].

Emotion "is a physiological departure from homeostasis that is subjectively experienced in strong feelings (as in love, hate, fear or desire) and manifests itself in neuro-muscular, respiratory, cardio-vascular, hormonal or other bodily changes preparatory to overt acts which may or may not be performed."

Homeostasis "is a tendency toward the maintenance of a relatively stable psychological condition of the individual with respect to contending drives, motivations and other psycho-dynamic forces."

Recent studies of anxiety and pain (14) have shown that "a threat to one's body or psychological well-being provokes a dramatic increase in cerebral metabolism and blood flow. Stress activates pathways in the brain and triggers the secretion of the hormone adrenaline which has a general arousal effect on the body."

Thus it would seem that all actual or apparent attacks on the self have visceral consequences: all result in a departure from homeostasis—a change in the internal environment of the person.

It is a matter of common experience that when we react emotionally in a situation, (*get up tight, lose our cool*), we lose perspective on the situation we are in.

"Strong emotions (15) blind us to a view of the situation as it is. We are attached to a particular view of it dictated by the emotion or desire. In this state we are not and cannot be open to what an inclusive view of the situation calls for from us. Instead we act on the basis of immediate sense data which is biased by our preoccupation with protecting, defending the self—just like any other animal intent on survival.''

''Thus, most basically, the problem created by a strong emotional reaction is that it precludes some possible options to action. One can only be open to the *Counsel of God*, (one's moral sense) if one is willing to accept that Counsel and move in any direction whatever. Jesus suggests a continuous choice, away from specific responses (as from emotions, desires, conditioned ideas and belief systems) toward a generalized *set* of the organism to find its fulfillment in identifying itself with whatever the moral sense indicates when it is not hanging on to a pre-determined, specific pattern of response. In such a homeostatic state, all responses are potential and the choice is made from a stable centre based on what emerges as the best for the moment.''

CHAPTER 23

Messianic Concepts in Relation to Jesus (4)

The early disciples of Jesus came to believe that he was the Christ of Jewish tradition. They expected him to reveal himself as such when he reached Jerusalem at the time of the Passover. These hopes and expectations were frustrated when Jesus was rejected by the religious leaders and executed. The disciples then dispersed, disillusioned and destitute. Their subsequent history is very vague though there are some legends (18).

Mark's account of the Jesus Story ends abruptly with the discovery that the tomb was empty—Jesus' body was no longer there. The accounts given by Matthew and Luke continue and explain the empty tomb in terms of a resurrection. They report post-resurrection appearances and there is a promise of a *second coming*. However the accounts given in the two books do not agree and it would seem that this material represents late additions to the story. They show how the belief of the early Christians changed from the conception of a political Christ held by the early followers of Jesus, *We hoped that it was he which would redeem Israel*, to a new belief; that though Jesus had been killed he had nevertheless been the Christ and having been resurrected, he was a Christ with a future. He would return *on the clouds of heaven in glory* and would function as a judge of righteousness.

This revised conception, apocalyptic in form, buttressed by prophetic utterances embedded in the Scriptures, became the basic belief of the early Christian church and acceptance of it as true was the prerequisite for membership in that community.

For the Jews generally, the notion of a crucified Christ was quite outrageous and their refusal to believe such a thing was, as Tuchman (7) says, the source of anti-semitism in the Church.

The origin of the Christian faith and of the church are thus seen to have grown out of a mistaken identification of Jesus with the traditional Jewish concept of the Christ. This identification persisted while he was alive in spite of his many efforts to deny it. And though the form of the concept changed to accommodate the fact of Jesus' death, the notion that he was the Christ persisted and continues to be believed to this day. *Believe on the Lord Jesus and thou shalt be saved* is still the message of some Christian sects.

Reflections of these Messianic (Christ) conceptions are to be found throughout the synoptic accounts of Jesus' life, especially in Matthew and Luke.

POLITICAL MESSIANISM (4)

¶ HE shall be great, and shall be called the Son of the Most High: and the Lord God shall give unto him the throne of his father David: and he shall reign over the house of Jacob for ever; and of his kingdom there shall be no end.

¶ Looking for the consolation of Israel.
Looking for the redemption of Jerusalem.

¶ Where is he that is born King of the Jews?
Where should the Christ be born?

¶ And thou Bethlehem, land of Judah,
Art in no wise least among the princes of Judah:
For out of thee shall come forth a governor,
Which shall be shepherd of my people Israel.

¶ Blessed be the Lord, the God of Israel;
For he hath visited and wrought redemption for his people,
And hath raised up a horn of salvation for us,
Salvation from our enemies, and from the hand of all that hate us;
To grant unto us that we being delivered out of the hand of our enemies
Should serve him without fear,
In holiness and righteousness before him all our days.

¶ Hosanna to the son of David! Blessed is the King that cometh in the name of the Lord, even the King of Israel. Blessed is the kingdom that cometh, the kingdom of our father David. Hosanna in the highest!

¶ Art thou the Christ, the Son of the Blessed?
 He says that he himself is Christ a king.
 Art thou the King of the Jews?
 Will ye that I release unto you the King of the Jews?
 What then shall I do unto him whom ye call the King of the Jews?
 Hail, King of the Jews!
 Ha! If thou art the King of the Jews, save thyself!
 THIS IS JESUS THE KING OF THE JEWS

APOCALYPTIC MESSIANISM

¶ REPENT ye; for the kingdom of heaven is at hand!
 The time is fulfilled, and the kingdom of God is at hand: repent ye, and believe in the gospel!
 Say unto them, The kingdom of God is come nigh unto you!
 Say unto them, Howbeit know this, that the kingdom of God is come nigh!

¶ I was not sent but unto the lost sheep of the house of Israel.

Go not into any way of the Gentiles, and enter not into any city of the Samaritans: but go rather to the loſt sheep of the house of Israel. And as ye go, preach, saying, The kingdom of heaven is at hand! When they persecute you in this city, flee into the next: for verily I say unto you, Ye shall not have gone through the cities of Israel, till the Son of man be come.

⁋ For the Son of man shall come in the glory of his Father with his angels; and then shall he render unto every man according to his deeds. Verily I say unto you, There be some of them that ſtand here, which shall in no wise taſte of death, till they see the Son of man coming in his kingdom.

⁋ Shall not God avenge his eleƈt, which cry to him day and night, and he is longsuffering over them? I say unto you, that he will avenge them speedily. Howbeit when the Son of man comēth, shall he find the faith on the earth?

⁋ In the regeneration when the Son of man shall sit on the throne of his glory, ye also shall sit upon twelve thrones, judging the twelve tribes of Israel.

⁋ There shall be terrors and great signs from heaven. There shall be signs in sun and moon and ſtars. The sun shall be darkened, and the moon shall not give her light, and the ſtars shall be falling from heaven, and the powers that are in the heavens shall be shaken. And then shall appear the sign of the Son of man in heaven. And they shall see the Son of man coming in clouds with great power and glory. And then shall he send forth the angels, and shall gather together his elect from the four winds, from the uttermost part of the earth to the uttermost part of heaven. Watch ye at every season, making supplication, that ye may prevail to escape all these things that shall come to pass, and to stand before the Son of man.

¶ Ye shall see the Son of man sitting at the right hand of the Power, and coming on the clouds of heaven.

¶ So shall it be in the end of the world: the angels shall come forth, and sever the wicked from among the righteous, and shall cast them into the furnace of fire: there shall be the weeping and gnashing of teeth.
So shall it be in the end of the world: the Son of man shall send forth his angels, and they shall gather out of his kingdom all things that cause stumbling, and them that do iniquity, and shall cast them into the furnace of fire: there shall be the weeping and gnashing of teeth. Then shall the righteous shine forth as the sun in the kingdom of their Father.

¶ When the Son of man shall come in his glory, and all the angels with him, then shall he sit on the throne of his glory: and before him shall be gathered all the nations: and he shall separate them one from another, as the shepherd separateth the sheep from the goats: and he shall set the sheep on his right hand, but the goats on the left. Then shall the King say unto them on his right hand, Come, ye blessed of my Father, inherit the kingdom prepared for you from the foundation of the world. Then shall he say also unto them on the left hand, Depart from me, ye cursed, into the eternal fire which is prepared for the devil and his angels. And these shall go away into eternal punishment: but the righteous into eternal life.

Jesus' own evaluation of the Messianic (Christ) concepts was an outcome of his personal experience at his baptism by John, § 2 and § 3. At that time Jesus came to understand that the coming of the Kingdom of God required that each individual deliberately choose to be ruled by God (good). The Kingdom of God came into existence for Jesus when he voluntarily turned over control of his life to God. Further, the Kingdom of God would grow by individual increments as other people came to accept God's rule in their lives. This conception of the manner of the coming of the Kingdom of God made the concept of the role of the Messiah (Christ) as God's emissary, redundant.

In § 80 of the text where Jesus was asked, *Is it lawful to give tribute to Caesar?* he replied, *Render unto Caesar the things that are Caesar's and unto God the things that are God's.* This was a negation of the political concept of the Christ's role since it asserted that paying tribute to Rome did not in fact mean that the payer was disloyal to

God. And this was saying that there was no need for the Christ to come to drive out the Romans. People could render unto God the loyalty they owed to God regardless of Rome's continued rule, § 24. See [23, first part].

Even a brief examination of the above apocalyptic material taken from the synoptic records will show that the language, the concepts and assumptions involved are quite foreign to the mind of Jesus. They are however quite consonant with the outlook, beliefs and expectations of the early Christian community. This material must therefore be regarded as late accretions to the *Jesus Story*, which developed among the early Christians. It expresses their belief that Jesus, though rejected and executed, had been resurrected and would soon return to function as judge of righteousness and to establish the Kingdom of God. See [23, second part].

The fallacy of the apocalyptic concept is seen as follows: When the King intervenes to set up a kingdom, the allegiance of the subjects is commanded rather than being freely given. The notion that somebody would descend from Heaven and assure that the Will of God be done on Earth, thus creating the Kingdom of God, was obviously quite contrary to Jesus' outlook for the subjects of such a kingdom, their loyalty commanded, would be slaves.

CHAPTER 24

Anthropomorphisms in The Language of Religion

Primitive man, fearful yet curious about the forces of Nature and chance happenings of every day life, found explanations in terms of spirits having powers like his own, though greater and, like himself, willing to make a deal—to accept a gift in return for protection.

In time, the spirits became gods; a mythology developed and a priest class appeared, claiming to be knowledgeable in the ways of the gods. Before long there was a ritual of homage—a form of worship evolved which was calculated to maintain a safe and even profitable relationship with the deities. And should that relationship be inadvertently broken, a procedure for its restoration was provided which, with priestly assistance was expected, though not guaranteed, to regain the god's favour. A comparative study of religions (9) reveals that man has always created his gods in his own idealized image—having all the powers he lacked but would like to have.

The case is no different with the Hebrew god Yahweh. That concept evolved as the culture of the Jews developed, exhibiting most human characteristics at one time or another over the long period of Jewish history. During the subsequent Christian era, Yahweh (God) became the object of theological speculation. He was shown to be imminent, omnipotent, omnipresent, omniscient and transcendent. Some of these attributes are well illustrated by the 17th Century Protestant definition of God in the Westminster Confession of Faith:

"There is but one living and true God, who is infinite in being and perfection, a most pure spirit, invisible, without body parts, or passions, immutable, immense, eternal, incomprehensible, almighty, most wise, most holy, most free, most absolute, working all things according to the counsel of his most immutable and most righteous will, for his own glory; most loving, gracious, merciful, long-suffering, abundant in goodness and truth, forgiving iniquity, transgressions and sin; the rewarder of them that diligently seek him; and withal most just and terrible in his judgments, hating all sin, and who will by no means clear the guilty."

This highly developed Christian theological formulation of the existence, nature and activity of God seems not to be very closely related to the Hebrew Yahweh from which it presumably derived. Yet it is no less anthropomorphic than its predecessor.

Clearly the God of orthodox Christianity—an objectively existing supernatural being, who is Creator, Father-figure, Intervenor, Protector and Punisher, is really the end-product of the evolution of those deities invented thousands of years ago by primitive peoples to satisfy their need for an explanation of natural phenomena.

Neither the Jewish Yahweh nor the Christian God were original or unique. It is relevant to recall that Zeus, the Greek sky-god, also a Father-figure who sent the rain, rewarded the good and punished the evil, was a contemporary of Yahweh. When occasion required it, Zeus cast his thunderbolts or flashed his Aegis. For the Romans, Jupiter played a similar role; the Germans had their Wodon who dwelt in Valhalla and had his Valkyries to do his bidding. Later, when these peoples became Christian, the name of the god changed but there was little if any essential difference in the new god's performance or alleged capability. The god—God, had his angels of many orders as messengers, demons, the Christ as special emissary and supernatural power with which to overcome Nature. Though a credit to the curiosity and imagination of our early ancestors, the existence of this supernatural god, God, is not supported by any objective evidence whatever. It is in fact pure fantasy. It has never existed save in the minds of its believers. It should have been exposed as a delusion long since and belief in it discouraged and denounced as superstition. Which it is. Instead, it has been deliberately maintained as TRUTH, taught to children and used to frighten, delude, victimize and coerce simple people.

If we now repudiate the notion of a supernatural God we will have taken a long step toward personal maturity though the consequences of such an exorcism may prove a burden to some. For when supernature goes, individual man, chance creature of the evolutionary process (12), is seen as he really is and has always been: alone in a neutral, purposeless Universe with nothing to lean upon but himself—no magic, no miracles and no free lunch. This fact, when faced, greatly unclutters the mind.

However to deny the existence of a supernatural God is not also to deny, for example, that many very ill people have recovered after calling upon God for aid. Nor does it assert that the moral and ethical values, which from time to time men have associated with God, have been unreal or worthless. Quite the contrary. Of course people have recovered from severe illnesses after asking for God's help, but Nature being the way it is, the cause of the effect is not to be discovered by postulating a supernatural order. It is not that easy. And the moral insights of the human race, accumulated over the millenia, while subject to critical appraisal to assess their present relevance, will be ignored only at great peril to us all.

Mythologies can be fascinating, but the truth is more beautiful and helpful. We can live, after a fashion, in a world of fantasy or face and accept the real, objective world. That acceptance requires that we be constantly on our guard against anthropomorphisms—especially those from our distant, racial past. For those being basic to our culture, permeate our language and literature and, unless we consciously repudiate them, they will subtly influence our thinking and behaviour.

In more recent times some Protestant theologians have tried to come to terms with some features of modern thought and this has given rise to a variety of new definitions of God. For example, Henry Nelson Wieman, (20):

"God is that feature of our total environment which most vitally affects the continuance and welfare of human life; that character of events to which man must adjust himself in order to attain the greatest goods and avoid the greatest evils; the most subtle and intimate complexity of environmental nature which yields the greatest good when right adjustment is made."

Wieman develops this concept more fully elsewhere (21). There he says:

"God is that which is supremely worthful for mankind. . . . The supremely worthful is that activity in our midst which shapes life toward the progressive attainment of mutual support and meaning. Supreme value then is growth of meaning in the world."

It should be noted that Wieman's God, Supreme Value, is not to be equated with the Universe or vested with supernatural power. Rather it is something which accrues—comes into being within groups of people when certain conditions are met. ". . . mutual support, mutual enhancement, and mutual meaning brings into a situation an organic

functioning which makes for continual increase of good and the progressive retirement of evil."
See also Monod (12), The Kingdom and the Darkness and Popper (23), The Third World.

Henry Nelson Wieman, Professor of Philosophy of Religion, The University of Chicago. Professor Wieman died in 1975 at the age of 90.

Jacques Monod (12), French Biochemist, awarded with André Lwoff and François Jacob, the Nobel Prize for Medicine and Physiology in 1965. Dr. Monod was the Director of the Pasteur Institute in Paris; he was Professor of the College of France and a foreign member of both the Royal Society and the National Academy of Sciences. Dr. Monod died in 1976.

Karl R. Popper (23), Emeritus Professor of Philosophy, University of London.

CHAPTER 25

The Meaning of the Phrase 'Will of God'

In Chapter 24, the anthropomorphic origin of the concepts of God, Christ, Supernatural etc. was examined. Here we examine certain words traditionally associated in our language with the symbolic word *God*. However, in throwing away a word we must take care not to discard, at the same time, the real human experience which was represented by that word in the mind of the user.

For example, John the Baptist, it is reported, heard *the word of God* which he obeyed. The Pharisees rejected *the Counsel of God*; Jesus urged people to do *the Will of God*. What would have been the meaning for these people of the *Word, Counsel, Will of God*?

The Phrase *Will of God* is clearly anthropomorphic. Man has a will, a purpose; ergo, God, a super-person has a will, a purpose, an intention for man. Man conveys his command or advice by speaking, so God, being like a man, must do the same. Man is aware of something telling, advising, urging him to act in a certain way. It must be God. Who else? So men reasoned but what was the reality? When Jesus used the word God, what was he referring to? Was it something objective, external, or was it something subjective, internal to himself, a voice which he personalized as Socrates did his Daemon?

Jesus did not think as his contemporaries did but that does not mean that he did not think. He was an original thinker. He went back to origins seeking the basic meanings of concepts and customs. But in expressing himself, he was of his Age. He had to use the language of his own time and culture. Nothing else was available to him. But if we examine some of Jesus' sayings—the words he used—we may find a clue to what was in his consciousness. For example: (1) ERV, 1881:

Lk. 4:8   *It is written, thou shalt worship the Lord thy God and him only shalt thou serve.*

Mat. 5:16 *Let your light so shine before all men that they may see your good works and glorify your Father.*

Mat. 5:37 *Let your speech be Yea, Yea, Nay, Nay and whatsoever is more than these is of evil.*

Mat. 5:44 *Love your enemies, do good to them that hate you.*

Mat. 6:1   *Take heed that ye do not your righteousness before men to be seen of them else ye have no reward with your Father.*

Lk. 6:9   *And Jesus said unto them, I ask you, is it lawful on the Sabbath to do good or*

MEANING OF THE PHRASE WILL OF GOD / 235

> *to do harm; to save a life or to destroy it?*
> Lk. 6:45 *The good man out of the good treasure of his heart bringeth forth that which is good.*
> Mar. 7:11 *If ye being evil knoweth how to give good gifts to your children, how much more shall your Father give good things to them that ask him?*
> Mk. 10:18 *And Jesus said unto him—Why callest thou me good? None is good save one, even God.*

In Summary: Clearly, Jesus is concerned with right action—doing what is right, what is good and with being honest and truthful. From the above quotations, his conception of God seems to have been anthropomorphic—God was like a man. However, the important point is that Jesus believed that God spoke to him, telling him what to do and he was obedient to that voice.

Apparently Jesus was confident that it was God's voice which enabled him to distinguish good from evil, right from wrong, in each situation. And he assumed that others would be similarly aided.

Now by definition [19], our word for that which discriminates between good and bad, right and wrong, is man's *moral sense*. And our word for that feeling of obligation to do what is good, what is right, to be honest and truthful, is *conscience*.

Thus, using *our language*, when Jesus urged people to do *the Will of God*, he was urging them to be guided by their conscience—do what your moral sense tells you is the right action to take in each situation.

It is surely legitimate to ask: Whence comes this moral sense and this conscience? There are two answers: Those who believe that man is the product of a *special creation* will say that man's moral sense is the voice of the Creator and that man's conscience is the Creator's means of needling and scolding him when he is or is inclined to be disobedient. This is clearly an anthropomorphic explanation. *No matter. The important thing is to obey.*

The other answer is given by those who believe that all animals including man are the product of a long process of evolution extending over many millions of years. Gradually over that time, animals developed a number of sensing mechanisms which have the function of telling the creature what is going on in its immediate physical environment. Data thus gathered by the animal's senses, after processing by its brain (central nervous system), triggers an appropriate neuromuscular response. This response is defined as *good*, *right* if it enables the animal to avoid danger, find food, find a mate and so go on living and reproducing. None of this sequence of events requires that the animal be *consciously aware* in the sense that man is aware, (12).

We are all familiar with this motor-individual in ourselves. Sherrington (11) gives an example:
"... Sense organ ... may or may not be a gateway to the mind: it is always a gateway to the motor-individual and its injunction to that individual may be to move or not to move." ... "What arises in the mind concurs with what is provoked by the motor-individual. Sometimes, however, in the experience of most of us, a sudden situation of urgency is met by our individual doing the right thing before the mind has grasped the situation. In the street's traffic we jump aside and leave the mind surprised that we have done so. We avert an unexpected blow before our thought has warned us. Our hand has caught the fragile cup before our mind seemed fully aware of its falling, let alone could issue orders for its saving."

Sherrington continues: ".... The motor-individual is driven from two sources—the world around it and the lesser world within. It can be regarded as a system which in virtue of its arrangement does a number of things and is so constructed that the world outside touches triggers for their doing. But its own internal condition has a say as to which of those things within limits it will do, and how it will do them. Its own internal condition is also initiator of some of its acts."

These quotations from Sherrington may help the reader to obtain a clearer picture of that aspect of man's behaviour which reflects the fact that like other animals, he is an integrated individual in the neuro-muscular field. One may also see that for man, mind, specifically conscious awareness, must have a role to play in selecting that course of action which would be most appropriate for him to take in each situation.

At the neuro-motor level, activity is motivated by one thing—"the zest of the living thing to go on living and to renew itself in a new life." At the level of conscious awareness, the motive may be the same—to go on living, but the objective, *living* now involves a different level of cognition and calls for action based on a broader, more inclusive array of information than that which is sufficient to trigger a reflex.

Traditionally, the word *moral* connotes codes of conduct—what one may or may not do—in relation to one's self or to other people. Our interest here is in what was there before the codes—what gave rise to the concepts of good, bad, right and wrong.

For those who accept the evolutionary explanation of the origin and development of life upon the earth, moral sense and conscience—whatever the actual mechanism of their functioning and of our awareness of them, must be seen to have had a natural origin. They seem to have the indispensable role of guiding the organism's behaviour in such a way as to maximize its probability of survival. Thus the moral sense discriminates between good and bad, right and wrong behaviour —not in an absolute sense but always relative to the welfare of the individual organism in each particular situation. On the neuro-motor level, this protection is applied automatically and in man, there is often no conscious awareness of it. On the level of consciousness, we are often aware of a *tension* (the conscience) urging us to accept a situation-evaluation already made and to act upon it. *This is the problem area.*

Recall that man's problem in any situation is: *What is the right thing for me to do now?* This question probably does not arise in animals other than man or his nearest relatives (12). It is an inescapable question for man because of his conscious awareness. He must review both his external and his internal situations before deciding what to do.

Unlike the motor-individual whose goals—to stay alive and to reproduce—are relatively readily reached because sense data triggers all the necessary responses, man's goals, though in some senses similar, seem to require careful consideration on the conscious level.

It is not easy to make up one's mind—to decide—what is the right thing to do in view of the many alternative scenarios which one's imagination simulates and presents—an activity which tends to slide into fantasy if one's attention slips. And there is the added complexity and claim of the accumulated experience of a lifetime which floods one's consciousness. One may feel vaguely that a certain choice of action would be appropriate but this feeling is immediately confronted by the compelling need to protect certain *sacred cows.*

We are all acquainted with the experience of not being able to recall a person's name—sometimes embarrassingly so—if the occasion is that we want to introduce that person to another. We say to ourselves—*I've known her for years—I've never liked her much, but I do know her name—it starts with a G. Whatever is it?* Then the thought comes —*Why not ask her?* But then—*After all these years I should admit that I don't know her name! Not bloody likely!* So we fumble a bit and manage by being only slightly impolite, to escape. Later that evening, when the feeling of embarrassment is gone and the dislike which was strengthened by the embarrassment, has faded, the name suddenly pops into consciousness. And surprise—it does not contain a G at all!

What is it that stands in the way—blocks insight? In this case, *dislike plus embarrassment at not knowing; plus refusal to admit; refusal to ask; plus insistence on G.* What to do?—remove the blocks. Surrender all the restrictions, reservations, likes and dislikes, special pleading. When I have *come clean* I may turn my problem over to my *internal computer* which has my whole record —all I know and have been and am is stored in its *memory bank.* We know from much experience that our computer—the central nervous system— serves very well at the level of the motor-individual. Surely it will cooperate at the conscious level also if it is not inhibited by limits and reservations consciously or unconsciously imposed on its operation.

Jesus' solution to the problem of central nervous system blockage was to affirm, consciously and persistently, over and over again, *Not my will but thine be done.*

Insight does not come just for the asking but if I am willing to remove myself completely and permanently from the *Picture Window,* the light shines through. That done, I must have *faith*—be confident that my own nervous endowment—my central nervous system—my brain, will perform and deliver the appropriate instructions to my consciousness just as it does to my arm and hand as I automatically and largely unconsciously reach for the falling cup in response to a milli-second glimpse of movement out of the corner of one eye! The arm is triggered to do the *right thing.* I also will be triggered to do the *right thing* if I am utterly willing to act on the insight when it comes.

I end this chapter with a final quote from Sherrington.* " . . . Let us see where we can first trace mind or where we last lose it. Does it not begin with the urge to live? Zest to live which is part and parcel of life? Is it not that all through? Becoming more sophisticated? The zest of the living thing to go on living and renew itself in a new life? The zest which implements the whole conduct of life; the zest which the whole conduct of life implements—at once an urge and a motive. No species of life without it. Innate, inalienable, impelling alike man and animalcule. A character which in the more than million-fold variety of nature's types, does not fail or falter in a single one. Individual minds of endless variety of type, reptile, fish, bee, octopus and . . . in all of them, whatever else, this constant trait—the drive to live and increase. We can call it zest and zest it often is, but who shall say where, traced along life's scale of forms receding from man's own, zest becomes blind drive, and drive retreats into mindless urge?"

Man is a creature of Nature. To affirm that fact is to affirm also man's zest for life and to seek its true satisfaction at whatever cost to oneself.

---

* (11) Sir Charles Sherrington, O.M., Waynflete Professor of Physiology in the University of Oxford; Nobel Prize for Physiology in 1932; President of the Royal Society of London. Sir Charles died in 1952 at the age of 95.

Bibliography

1. English Bible, English Revised Version, (ERV 1881).
2. B. H. Streeter, *The Four Gospels*, MacMillan, 1930.
3. H. B. Sharman, *The Records of the Life of Jesus*, 1917, now Sequoia Seminar, Palo Alto, Ca.
4. H. B. Sharman, *Jesus as Teacher*, Student Edition, 1935, Sequoia Seminar, as above.
5. The Jerusalem Bible, (J. B. 1966), Doubleday.
6. The New English Bible, (NEB), New Testament, Second Ed. 1970.
7. Barbara Tuchman, *A Distant Mirror*, Alfred A. Knopf, 1979.
8. William Shakespeare, *Henry Fourth*, Pt 1, Act 3, Line 52 et seq.
9. Geoffry Parrinder, *The World's Living Religions*, Pan, 1974.
10. Columbia Encyclopedia, Third Edition, 1963.
11. Sir Charles Sherrington, *Man on His Nature*, Cambridge Univ. Press, 1951.
12. Jacques Monod, *Chance and Necessity*, Vintage Books, 1972.
13. G. F. Moore, *Judaism in the First Centuries of the Christian Era*. Vols. I and II, Schocken Books, 1971.
14. Lassen, Ingvar and Skinhøs, *Brain Function and Blood Flow*, Scientific American, October 1978.
15. Frances Warnecke Horn, *I Want One Thing*. DeVorss, 1981.

16. G. and C. Merriam Co., *Webster's Third International Dictionary*, 1976.
17. W. K. Clifford, *The Ethics of Belief*, reprinted in Walter Kaufman's *Religion from Tolstoy to Camus*, Harper and Row, 1964.
18. B. H. Streeter, *The Primitive Church*, MacMillan, 1929.
19. Josephus, *The Jewish War*, Translated by Williamson, Penguin Classics, 1959.
20. H. N. Wieman, *The Wrestle of Religion with Truth*, MacMillan, 1927.
21. H. N. Wieman and B. E. Meland, *American Philosophies of Religion*, Willett, Clark Co., N.Y. 1936.
22. A. Schweitzer, *The Quest of the Historical Jesus*, A. C. Black, London, 1926.
23. Karl Popper, *Objective Knowledge*, Oxford, 1972.
24. G. A. Williamson, *The World of Josephus*, Secker and Warburg, 1964.
25. H. B. Sharman, *Son of Man and Kingdom of God*, Harper and Bros., 1943.
26. H. B. Sharman, *The Teaching of Jesus About the Future*, Univ. of Chicago Press, 1909.
27. *Acts of the Apostles*, (1), 5:34-37.
28. Emil Schürer, *The Literature of the Jewish People in the Time of Jesus*, Schocken Books. 1972.
29. Emil Schürer, *A History of the Jewish People in the Time of Jesus*, Schocken Books, 1961.
30. Hans Küng, *On Being a Christian*, Collins, 1978.
31. Edward Schillebeeck, *Jesus—An Experiment in Christology*. Seabury Press, 1979.
32. Jaroslav Pelikan, *The Christian Tradition*, Vol 1, Univ of Chicago Press, 1971.
33. Henry Chadwick, *The Early Church*, Pelican, 1967.
34. Solomon Grayzel, *A History of the Jews*, Mentor Books, 1947.

35. Elaine Pagels, *The Gnostic Gospels*, Random House, 1979.
36. H. G. Wells, *An Outline of History*, Garden City Publishing Co., 1921.
37. *This One Thing—A Tribute to Henry Burton Sharman*, The Student Christian Movement of Canada, 1959.
38. Duncan Howlett, *The Critical Way in Religion*, Prometheus Books, 1980.

Dr. Sharman was the author of ten books—the first in 1896, the last in 1945—his eightieth year. All dealt with the Records of the Life of Jesus.

The copyright to most of Dr. Sharman's books is held by The Sequoia Seminar, Inc., 222 High Street, Palo Alto, CA. 94301.